JOHNNY WON'T HIT TODAY

A Cricketing Biography of
J. W. H. T. Douglas

JOHNNY WON'T HIT TODAY

A Cricketing Biography of
J. W. H. T. Douglas

DAVID LEMMON

London
GEORGE ALLEN & UNWIN
Boston   Sydney

George Allen & Unwin (Publishers) Ltd,
40 Museum Street, London WC1A 1LU, UK

George Allen & Unwin (Publishers) Ltd,
Park Lane, Hemel Hempstead, Herts HP2 4TE, UK

Allen & Unwin Inc.,
9 Winchester Terrace, Winchester, Mass 01890, USA

George Allen & Unwin Australia Pty Ltd,
8 Napier Street, North Sydney, NSW 2060, Australia

First published in 1983

British Library Cataloguing in Publication Data

Lemmon, David
  Johnny won't hit today.
1. Douglas, J.W.H.T.   2. Cricket players—
England—Biography
I. Title
796.35'8'0924   GV915.D/
ISBN 0-04-796076-0

Set in 11 on 13 point Garamond by Bedford Typesetters Ltd
and printed in Great Britain
by Billing and Sons Ltd, London and Worcester

Contents

List of Illustrations

Credits

BBC Hulton Picture Library 2, 3, 6, 8, 9, 10, 11, 12, 13; MCC 5, 7, 14.

Preface

The author is indebted to many people for their assistance in the compilation of this book. All have been so generous in their help and time. Among them are Peter Edwards and Essex CCC; Mike Marshall; Jack Rollin; Norman Epps, editor of the Corinthian Casuals magazine; S. G. Brabner; Ken Harrison; Jim Coldham; David Frith; A. G. Waterman; T. N. Pearce; Norman Simson and the Spalding Gentlemen's Society; Leslie Newnham, who has given much help and compiled the statistics; Mrs Phillips and the Amateur Boxing Association; G. O. Allen; Ken Porter and Southend CC; R. J. Swain and Wanstead CC; P. P. Shorter, the secretary of Theydon Bois Golf Club; Bob Dunn; Thomas Beale; John Chandler; Mr Hinde of Felsted School; Mr A. E. Eggleston, CBE, the headmaster of Felsted School; and countless others who, like Roy Scott Moncrieff, wrote me letters of warmth and memory or passed me words of encouragement.

David Lemmon
Leigh-on-Sea, 1982

1
Father and Son

'He stood with his foot resting on the little body, suddenly musing, filled with the desire that his son should be like him, and should have sons like him, to people the earth. It is the strongest desire that can come to a man – if it comes to him at all – stronger even than love or the desire for personal immortality. All men vaunt it, and declare that it is theirs; but the hearts of most are set elsewhere. It is the exception who comprehends that physical and spiritual life may stream out of him forever.'

(E. M. Forster: *Where Angels Fear to Tread*)

John H. Douglas was one of those exceptions. Like Forster's hero, Gino, he saw in his children the continuation of himself, and he was fortunate that his children responded to his ambitions for them.

His own life can be measured as a success. He built up a highly profitable business, centred in Bishopsgate, which was concerned with the import of timber used mainly for the construction of staves in which cement was encased.

He was a sportsman of note. He first won the Queensberry amateur middleweight championship in 1875, when he was 22 years old, and he won it again in 1876 and 1877. As a representative of the Mincing Lane Boxing and Athletic Club, he served on the committee of the Amateur Boxing Association for several years, his voice a strong one in the proposing of motions and the refusing of reinstatements. He dealt firmly with any transgression of the rules of the association. On 4 April 1905, he spoke vehemently that the application for affiliation by the Bow and Bromley Cycling and Athletic Club be refused, as their rules did not contain the definition of an amateur required by the rules of the ABA. 18 months later, he proposed that G. Jessup be suspended for one month for boxing at an unauthorised meeting and he relentlessly pursued the report from Scotland Yard that they had received an anonymous letter stating that at a meeting in Northampton a boxer had received five pounds.

He was a brusque man, a man of controlled passion who wanted his own way and generally got it. In every aspect of his life he became a powerful man, one who came to have some say in the destiny of others. In November 1906, he was unanimously elected president of the ABA in succession to George Vize, who had held the office since 1893. J. H. Douglas was to remain as president for 18 years. No-one has held the office longer.

His passion for cricket was as great as his passion for boxing and he served as chairman of the Club Cricket Conference. Until 1900, he and his family lived at Clapton, on the Middlesex side of the Middlesex/Essex border, and he was a captain and administrator of the Clapton Cricket Club. Here it was that he claimed to have discovered the great Walter Mead and introduced him to Essex for whom he played from 1894 to 1913.

It was at Clapton, on 3 September 1882, that his first son, John William Henry Tyler, was born. The boy inherited much from the father, in ability, in temperament, and in the unwillingness to admit defeat. The father lodged in the boy a passion to succeed at sport, and a strong affinity was welded between the two which transcended the father–son relationship and which lasted until their deaths.

In his days with Clapton Cricket Club, J. H. Douglas met

2

and became close friends with a London schoolmaster, A. S. Hatt. Hatt was a fine club cricketer renowned for his quick eye and supple wrists. He played for Clapton, the Stoics and North Middlesex and earned a reputation for his ability to play fast bowling. Douglas had a great admiration for Hatt and when Hatt moved to Lincolnshire to become head-master of Moulton Grammar School, near Spalding, he entrusted to him his elder son for the preparatory years of his education.

Johnny Douglas arrived at Moulton in January 1895, the term after Hatt had been appointed headmaster. He arrived in the company of another new boy from London, Harold Milton. The two boys made an immediate impact at the school on the soccer field. For several years the matches between the day-boys and boarders had been closely-fought contests; from the day that Douglas and Milton arrived, the boarders dominated.

Shortly after the first world war, an appreciation of Douglas appeared in *The Moultonian*, the school magazine, under the signature of 'J.G.W.' and he recalled:

'There were giants in those days' on the playing field at Moulton, as surely as ever there were in the ancient days of Noah; and the most redoubtable of all those giants was Johnny Douglas.

Nor were the prospects of the day-boys any rosier when the summer term came round. Though we had excellent bowlers, the boarders had more excellent batsmen, and again we were the victims of the same dreadful pair from London. Should anyone still further dispute their supremacy, and think to get level with them by a victory with the gloves, the last word still rested with the boarders, the last blow fell – from Douglas – on the body of the too presumptuous day-boy.

Douglas himself always spoke highly of Moulton Grammar

School, which amalgamated with Spalding Grammar School in the 1930s, saying that he was lucky to have a very good cricket master and a good ground. For its part, the school regarded Douglas as its most distinguished old boy and when he became captain of England a tree in the grounds of the school on which he had carved his initials, J.W.H.T.D., became something of a shrine for the younger boys. Until the outbreak of the first world war both he and Douglas senior always made an appearance in Moulton's cricket week.

In May 1897, Johnny Douglas arrived at Felsted School in Essex. He was given a place in the house of Rev. E. Gepp. The academic term which began in September 1897 saw him under the tutorship of Mr V. C. Stutfield and he finished second in the list of the Modern Middle Fourth. The following term he won the Lower School Set One Mathematics Prize. It is the sole record of any academic achievement in his school years; of his sporting prowess, the records are legion.

Old Douglas had sworn his son to sport like a young Hannibal, and by the time he arrived at Felsted the boy was well drilled, well equipped and eminently correct in half-a-dozen sports. In May 1898, he won the three-quarter mile race on Sports Day. 'Douglas ran with great judgment, and coming with a fine spurt in the straight, won splendidly. Time 4 minutes, 3 seconds.' In second place was A. M. Clark and in third place I. F. Fairbairn-Crawford, one of four Olympic runners produced by Felsted at the turn of the century.

A few weeks later Douglas was partnering Partridge in the final of the junior fives tournament, which they won with ease, and of his cricket it was being written: 'Douglas and Johnstone are both promising, especially the former, who has the makings of a really good bowler, and both of them are very fair bats.'

Not all shared this view, some suggesting that the strength of his bowling hid a weakness in batting. The sharpest, most succinct assessment, was to come years later by R. C. Robertson-Glasgow, who said of him that he was 'by nature a bowler, by force of character a batsman'. P. P. Braithwaite, the school cricket captain for 1898, selected Douglas as an all-rounder, however, and the results proved him justified. In the match against Chelmsford at Chelmsford, on 21 May, he showed characteristic determination: 'The rest, with the exception of Douglas, who played pluckily, gave little trouble, and the whole side was out for 84.'

The next match was against the Old Boys, a 12-a-side game which was lost by one wicket. Douglas took 6 for 47. There followed the annual match with Essex Club & Ground. Douglas senior opened for the county representatives and was caught at slip by Johnstone off Douglas junior's bowling for 1 before the rains came.

His first year in the XI proved to be a good one with the ball, 23 wickets at 15.65 runs each, but a poor one with bat, only 49 runs at 6.12 an innings. His father was a regular visitor at the school, anxious to see that his son's head was not turned by his precocious talent, the talent which he had fostered so eagerly. He placed emphasis on the development of character and in this he was at one with the headmaster, H. A. Dalton, a man of remarkable energy and a cricket fanatic.

With the cricket season at an end, Johnny Douglas now turned his attention to other sports. He played right-back for his house soccer team and left-back for the school second XI although by the end of the season he had played in the first XI.

On 8 March 1899, he won the school lightweight championship, beating King-Smith by half a point, the result being in doubt until the last. He had been taught the finer points of boxing in his infancy and from the first he impressed as a clean hitter with an impenetrable defence. On Friday 24 March, he was at Aldershot for the Public Schools' Gymnastic, Boxing and Fencing Competition. Each one of his opponents was bigger than he was, but he won the title easily and was considered to be the best boxer of the tournament. A year later, in defence of his title, he was confined to a sick bed until four days before the tournament. Although unwell, he won his first bout, but he was so weak that he was forced to retire from the competition. He returned in 1901 to claim his title again.

The 1899 cricket season saw Douglas come to fruition as a schoolboy bowler. In the early part of the season success followed success. He had 5 for 39 against T. N. Perkins' XI, 7 for 58 against Chelmsford CC and bowled his father for 20 when Essex Club & Ground visited Felsted. Later, Douglas senior brought his own XI to play the school and retired when he reached 55; his son took five wickets.

Johnny was now also being used as an opening batsman, scoring 15 and 55 not out against Merchant Taylors' as well as taking 5 for 80. He averaged 23.92 with the bat, but it was as a bowler that he dominated with 56 wickets at 15.05 runs apiece. There was, however, in *The Felstedian*'s assessment of the season, a warning to Johnny Douglas which he would not, or could not, heed:

> A good bowler; began the season well, but latterly, owing no doubt to the fact that he never gave himself any rest, fell off somewhat. A good steady bat, cutting and driving well; fair field, but not quite quick enough for the slips.

In truth, he did not know the meaning of rest, ever searching for some means of physical expression, driven by a will to win and a belief that he could bring about victory. All his life he filled 'the unforgiving minute with sixty seconds' worth of distance run'. Supremely fit, and dedicated to the ideal of fitness, he was never quick in any sport. Quickness of movement is the gift given to the natural athlete and J. W. H. T. Douglas was an athlete by perseverance and ambition, not by nature.

In the soccer season he forced his way into the first team as a winger, but the comment is astute:

> Douglas at outside-left plays a hard persevering game; though very slow, he centres and passes well. . . . was slow, and did not keep far enough out on the line. . . . Too slow to make an ideal outside-right, could pass very well, but much too inclined to go back with the ball instead of forward.

Nevertheless, he held his place in the first team for most of the season, dropping back in defence for an heroic rearguard action when injury reduced the side to ten men on occasions. The Felsted fixture list was an interesting one at the time, for they numbered among their opponents such teams as Chelmsford, Richmond Association, St John's, Leatherhead, and Ipswich Town, although it is doubtful if the last was quite the force in 1900 that it has become in recent years.

Soccer continued at Felsted until the first world war, when rugby was introduced. The Old Felstedians played their first rugby match in November 1919, and a few days later, the Old Felstedians Football Club was dissolved. This did not entirely suit John Douglas. He had continued his soccer career with the Old Felstedians after he left school, when cricket tours permitted, and he had a passionate interest in the game, as he did in every sport he played. Before the first world war, he played for the Casuals on occasions, and he played for the Corinthians, the most famous amateur soccer club of the time, both before and after the war.

His last games for the Corinthians were in November 1919, at the age of 37. He played left-half against RMA

Woolwich (H. M. Morris, who was to succeed him as Essex captain, was also in the side), in goal against Cambridge University at Queen's Club, and at right-half in the return match at Cambridge. He had played for England in one of the Internationals arranged by the Amateur Football Alliance between 1907 and 1913. The AFA was formed in 1907 following a dispute with the FA over the control of amateur football. From 1907 to 1913, those affiliated to one association were forbidden to play with or against those affiliated to the other, so both the FA and the AFA arranged amateur internationals. It is accepted that John Douglas, as an Old Felstedian, played for the AFA England team on at least one occasion, but the AFA's records were destroyed in the second world war and it is not known against whom he played, or when.

The teams selected to represent Great Britain in the 1912 Olympic Games were chosen from those sides affiliated to the FA, which meant the exclusion of many of the very best amateur players whose allegiance was to clubs like the Corinthians, affiliated to the AFA. John Douglas was appalled by this situation and was a signatory to a letter published in *The Times* on 11 September 1911, imploring the FA and the AFA to co-operate in the selection of the Great Britain team for the 1912 Olympic Games in Stockholm. Other signatories to the letter included Lord Harris, J. R. Mason, who had captained Kent until 1902, and Stanley Christopherson.

When the Old Felstedians FC was dissolved Douglas was turned 37, but in a last defiant gesture he captained them in the Arthur Dunn Cup in 1920. They lost to Highgate's Old Cholmondeleians; his career, and the playing days of Old Felstedians FC, were over.

In June 1900, Douglas was made a prefect at Felsted and gained a reputation as a disciplinarian. It was a reputation that he was to keep for the rest of his life. He had a highly

successful cricket season, scoring his first century for the
school and averaging 43.46 with the bat. He took 34 wickets
at 17.55 each, and

> has been the mainstay of the team in batting, only failing to
> obtain double figures three times. Plays very straight, and
> has a beautiful cut, though at times rather slow. Has hardly
> done himself justice as a bowler, though he has been
> extremely useful. Rather an uncertain field.

Douglas senior continued his regular visits to the school and
scored 54 retired when he brought his own XI to face the
side of which his son was a member.

In the winter, John Douglas added a hockey colour to his
colours for cricket, soccer, gymnasium and fives. As a
hockey player he was deemed to be one who 'did not go
straight enough to make a good centre. A clever dribbler,
but weak in the circle.' He was still a member of the soccer
team, 'a clever and resourceful player. At times inclined to
dally too long with the ball.' He performed in the Prefects'
Annual Entertainment, playing the part of Dr Planus 'well'
in *Furnished Apartments*, a short sketch on the lines of *Box
and Cox*.

He dominated the boxing at the school. At Aldershot, in
the Public Schools' Championships of 1901, he knocked out
his opponent in the final. In the second round he had beaten
P. R. Reid of Haileybury, who was a stone heavier than
himself. Those were the type of odds he relished.

After his distinguished record as a games player in general,
and as a cricketer in particular, it can be presumed that
Douglas would have anticipated being elected cricket captain
for the 1901 season. If this was the case, then he was to be
disappointed. The elected captain was E. W. Smith. On the
eve of the season, however, Smith fell ill and did not play a
single game. Douglas took over the captaincy. It was a

portent. Throughout his career Douglas was to achieve captaincy by default. On the one occasion when he was given the job unopposed, he was to be dismissed after two losing matches.

By 1901, in the mature schoolboy cricketer could be seen the clear shape of the man who was to become a forceful personality in international cricket for two decades. He was 'a steady and reliable bat, rather lacking in forcing powers. A useful bowler and a hard worker in the field. Captained the team with great success.' His solid batting, it seems, was always at its best when things were going badly. His final figures, 515 runs in 11 innings at an average of 64.37 and 33 wickets at 16.10, were impressive.

The Douglas link with Felsted was to continue, for in the term that John Douglas left, his younger brother, Cecil Herbert, arrived. C. H. 'Pickles' Douglas played county cricket, but he was to become most renowned as a boxing referee, a position which John Douglas himself often occupied for the Amateur Boxing Association in later years and which he occupied annually at matches and competitions at Felsted. It was said of him that he always gave praise where praise was due, and had a word of congratulation for the winner and a word of encouragement for the loser, and a piece of expert advice for each.

He left Felsted in July 1901. He was two months short of his nineteenth birthday and his academic career had not marked him out for university. His school career had been sport and the discipline and application which he and his father attached to sport. His nickname among the other boys was 'Pro'. It was a name awarded part in admiration, part in envy and part, perhaps, in the belief that there was something not totally acceptable, not completely gentlemanly, in Douglas' ruthless dedication.

2
For Essex

In 1900, the Douglas family had moved to Wanstead and J. H. Douglas became as prominent in Wanstead Cricket Club as he had been at Clapton. Known as 'the Old Man' or 'the Guv'nor', he used his wealth and position to enhance the club and its reputation. He was responsible for having the club wicket entirely re-laid. Turf was purchased from the old Tottenham cricket ground and several trucks of Nottingham marl were laid under the supervision of the Essex County groundsman Freeman, uncle of the Kent leg-break bowler and of the Essex opening bat. Most of the expense was borne by 'the Old Man'.

One of the club events which he encouraged was the annual ladies' match on the last Wednesday in June, the ladies batting with bats and the men with broomsticks, left-handed. Among the ladies, one of the fiercest competitors was Dolly Douglas, the sister of Cecil and Johnny, an overarm medium-pacer of no mean ability.

The Douglas family was committed to Wanstead Cricket Club and 'the Old Man' captained them from 1907 to 1921 when he retired and was elected president, a position he held until his death. His reign as captain was one of vitality, enthusiasm and driving ambition. In summer, there would be nets before breakfast and in the evenings the ground swarmed with those at practice.

Johnny Douglas first played for Wanstead in 1901, shortly after leaving Felsted, and last played for them in 1929 in a midweek match when he defended dourly and saved the side from defeat. In 1902, he averaged 82 in his eight innings for Wanstead and took 17 wickets at 12.29 each. His most memorable contribution was in the match against Buckhurst Hill on 19 July when he and N. S. Snell put on over 200 for the first wicket, Douglas' contribution being 116 not out.

He had made his debut for Essex a year earlier, a few weeks after leaving school. It is fallaciously believed that his selection for Essex came about because his father exerted pressure that his son should be included in the side, but by the time he was invited to play three matches in August, J. W. H. T. Douglas had earned his chance. He had a good record at Felsted and had played two games for Essex 2nd XI against Middlesex, getting wickets in both games, scoring 145 at Leyton and carrying his bat through the innings at Lord's.

His debut for the first team, against Yorkshire at Leyton, was less auspicious. Yorkshire were formidable opposition: as Douglas Jardine was to observe later and as Denzil Batchelor was to remark in his memorable little biography of C. B. Fry, if you wanted to assess a batsman, 'it was only necessary to keep your eye on how he fared against Yorkshire.' Yorkshire won the title that year, as they had done the year before and were to do the year after, and George Hirst took 183 wickets, 12 of them in that match at Leyton which Yorkshire won by an innings although they only made 104. Hirst had just perfected his famous swerve and it twice proved too much for Johnny Douglas, bowled for 0 in each innings.

He failed to score at Clifton, too, when the side travelled down to meet Gloucestershire, but he hit 61 not out against Derbyshire at Chesterfield in his third match. He was not asked to bowl in any of the three matches. More disappointingly, he was not asked to play in 1902.

At the end of the 1901 season he played for the Cross Arrows against George Robey's XI at Lord's. In those September days of 1901, the Cross Arrows' matches were played on the great ground itself and not, as today, on the Nursery practice ground wicket. Tom Richardson was to have played for Robey's XI, but he withdrew from the side and his place was taken by Jack Hobbs. It was the first confrontation between Douglas and 'the Master'. On this occasion Hobbs scored 55, but he gained a deep respect for Douglas, whom he considered to be one of the best bowlers he ever faced. They were to have many intriguing contests over the next quarter of a century.

Douglas had been well coached at Moulton Grammar School and later at Felsted, where he was helped by one of the masters, T. N. Perkins, and by the professional coach, Harrison, who had played for Nottinghamshire. His batting, however, was obviously below the standard required by first-class cricket when he made his debut for Essex. He was not a natural batsman, and what he achieved, he achieved through application. That application was acquired and practised in his days with London County Cricket Club.

London County Cricket Club was formed in 1899 with W. G. Grace as captain and secretary. It was granted first-class status in 1900 and played some 64 first-class matches before it was disbanded at the end of the 1904 season. J. W. H. T. Douglas played for London County in the last two years of the club's existence. In 19 innings for them he scored 275 runs and took 15 wickets. He shared in two century stands for the seventh wicket: 122 with W. G. Grace against Gloucestershire at Crystal Palace in 1903, and 185 with E. H. D. Sewell against Surrey, also at Crystal Palace, in 1904. It was in the games with Grace's XI that Douglas learned to apply himself, and it was in these games that he turned himself into an obdurate batsman.

He returned to county cricket with Essex at the end of June 1903, when he batted no. 6, scoring 19 and 0 not out and helping to inflict upon Sussex one of the two defeats that they suffered in the Championship in which they finished second. He bowled his first overs in county cricket and took his first Championship wicket when he bowled Joe Vine, who was later to play his only Test matches under Douglas' captaincy.

In that first half-season of Championship cricket Douglas was slow to develop. His 40 not out against Nottinghamshire at Leyton represented his highest score, his 17 innings producing only 185 runs at an average of 13.33. He took 21 wickets at 26.19 runs each, and against Kent at Canterbury he took five wickets in an innings for the first time, 5 for 63. Kent won the match, though, their first victory over Essex at Canterbury.

The following season showed little progress had been made, and it was not until 1905 that Douglas made his first real advance, when he took 35 wickets and topped the Essex bowling averages. This was the year in which he exacted his first revenge on Yorkshire by taking five wickets in eight balls, all clean bowled, at Leyton. He bowled Tunnicliffe with a slow yorker. It was the fifth ball of the over and the teams went to lunch when the wicket fell. On the resumption he bowled Hirst with the remaining ball of the over and in his next over he bowled Rhodes, Haigh and Myers with the last three deliveries. It was the first hat-trick ever accomplished by an Essex player, and years afterwards, he remembered it as the game which afforded him the keenest pleasure. There were those among his friends who believed that Yorkshire always brought the best out of Johnny Douglas because, like A. E. W. Mason's hero in *Four Feathers*, he was always striving to correct an initial unjustified indignity. Yorkshire played cricket in a way that Johnny Douglas understood, hard and fair.

Whatever advances he made in cricket in 1905, they were as nothing compared to those he made in boxing, for it was in this year that he won the amateur middleweight championship of Great Britain.

The Douglas family had a commanding influence on amateur boxing in the Edwardian period. As we have seen, old Douglas was president of the ABA from 1906 to 1924, when he sent a letter of resignation to the Annual General Meeting. His resignation was accepted with deep regret and he was presented with an illuminated address and elected a life member of the association. Johnny, 'Pickles' and Douglas senior all served on the council and acted as judges.

Johnny's greatest achievement in the ring was to come at the Olympic Games in London in 1908, when he won the Olympic middleweight title. His opponent in the final was the Australian, 'Snowy' Baker, and they contrived one of the greatest bouts in Olympic history, indeed in the history of amateur boxing. 'It was,' said *The Times*, 'one of the most brilliant exhibitions of skilful boxing allied to tremendous hitting ever seen.' At the end of the three rounds, neither the judges nor the referee could separate the two boxers and give a decision, and so, for what is believed to be the only time in the history of the Olympic boxing tournament, the contestants were asked to box an extra round. At the end of the extra round, the difference between the two was still minute, but the gold medal was awarded to Douglas.

It was the pinnacle of his boxing career although there is a folk tale, which can be neither substantiated nor refuted, that he fought the professional, Tommy Burns, behind closed doors at the 'Blue Anchor' at Shoreditch. It is unlikely that this tale is true as such a contest, if discovered, would have had serious and scandalous implications for Johnny and his father, a rigorous upholder of the rules of the

ABA. On the other hand, the story has a flavour which is very much in keeping with the Regency characters of both men. There was something 'hell fire' about the Douglases.

At the beginning of the 1906 season, Essex faced a crisis. Walter Mead had not played for two seasons since being in dispute with the club after he had requested an increase in his winter pay. To say the least, the matter had been handled badly. On top of this woe, support had been poor and the county had had a miserable season in 1905 so that extinction was by no means improbable. Happily, the dispute with Mead was settled, the crowd at Leyton gave increased support and the team prospered. For the first time Douglas played a full season, and for the first time he scored over 1000 runs in all matches although his first hundred eluded him. He had a growing reputation as a dour, defensive batsman. At Canterbury in 1905, he had batted for an hour and a half against Kent, scoring 8 not out and saving the game for Essex, but in the following season, he began to show other qualities.

His batting was ever practical rather than aesthetic, but he played a memorable innings against Middlesex at Leyton, hitting his highest score of the season, 98, in the second innings. In the first innings he had batted at no. 6 and Essex took a narrow lead, Douglas having bowled superbly to take 6 for 40. He was less successful when Middlesex batted again, and the visitors made 346. This left Essex the very stiff task of making 341 to win, which seemed highly improbable since on the opening day, 20 wickets had fallen while 268 runs were scored. Fane and Douglas began the Essex second innings on the second evening and they had reached 92 before the close of play. The following morning they took their stand to 208 before Douglas was caught by Tarrant off Trott two short of his century. He had played what *Wisden* described as 'the best innings of his career', and Essex went

16

on to win by 7 wickets, one of the most remarkable victories of the season.

In all matches in 1906, Johnny Douglas took 93 wickets, so coming close to the coveted double for the first time. He had some remarkable days. Against Kent, the eventual champions, at Tunbridge Wells, for example, he took nine wickets in the match. In the first innings, he bowled one bizarre over in which James Seymour played-on off a no-ball, Huish was caught off a no-ball, Seymour was dropped by Perrin off the next ball and Huish bowled by the next.

His outstanding bowling performance of the season was in the match against Leicestershire at Southchurch Park, Southend. This was the first occasion that county cricket was played on the ground which now boasts one of the best wickets in England, and by three o'clock on the second afternoon, the Tuesday, the game had seemingly reached stalemate with each side having completed one innings and Leicestershire leading by 23 runs. Just over an hour later, Leicestershire were an all but beaten side. In 13 overs and 5 balls of relentlessly accurate bowling, Douglas took 8 wickets for 33 runs. He had moved the ball appreciably (although *Wisden* referred to him as getting 'spin on the ball') and was virtually unplayable. Rain prevented any more play until two o'clock on the Wednesday, but Essex duly won by five wickets. To commemorate the event, a local enthusiast wrote out a large scorecard and decorated it with the coloured badges of the two counties. It hangs in the pavilion at Southchurch Park, the home of Southend Cricket Club, to this day.

In December 1906, Johnny Douglas went on his first overseas tour when he was a member of the MCC team which Captain Wynyard took to New Zealand. Wynyard, in fact, was injured in the third match of the tour and the side was led in the remaining matches by C. E. de Trafford.

First-class cricket had been played in New Zealand as far

17

back as 1864, but the advance towards international status did not begin until 'Plum' Warner captained a side got together by Lord Hawke on a tour of the country in 1902–03. That side had proved too strong for the local opposition and in 1906, the MCC's venture was on much more modest lines. They sent an all-amateur side. 'Professional bowling was dispensed with and no attempt was made to secure such powerful batting as before.' In an interview for A. C. MacLaren's *World of Cricket* a few years later, Douglas put the standard in New Zealand in 1906 on a par with the standard he encountered in America and Canada a year later. The MCC side was beaten only twice in 16 matches, once by Canterbury, when Douglas was not in the side, and once by the New Zealand XI in the second and final 'Test'.

In the two 'Test' matches, Douglas performed nobly, scoring 40 in the first, and 18 and 37 in the second. His bowling was even more impressive with figures of 5 for 56 and 4 for 51, and 7 for 49 and 5 for 76. It was the climax of a splendid tour in which he topped both the batting and the bowling averages in the first-class matches, scoring just under 400 runs and taking 50 wickets.

He returned to another successful season with Essex. Charles McGahey had succeeded Fane as captain and Essex enjoyed a season much the same as they had had in 1906. There was no decline in support and the mood was generally optimistic. In all matches, Douglas again came close to the double, taking 90 wickets and scoring 902 runs.

Essex were twice beaten by the South African touring side, in May and August, and Douglas produced one of his renowned overs of eccentricity in the second encounter when he bowled three no-balls, one of which bowled S. J. Snooke, the second of which the same batsman hit for four and the third of which bowled J. H. Sinclair.

These matches were the first in which he met the formidable South African leg-spin and googlies of White, Faulkner, Schwarz and Vogler. It was not a type of bowling which Douglas ever found easy to master. Although he was a champion boxer and had reached the heights in several sports, he was never quick on his feet, nor particularly agile in movement. What he achieved, he had had to work at, and the art of dealing with the leg-break was something which was for ever to remain something of a mystery to him. The rising ball he played with courage and an ease that many envied; the guile of the leg-spinner and googly bowler left him leaden-footed and bemused.

Undoubtedly, Douglas' best match in 1907 was the one against Kent at Leyton when he took 6 for 69 and 7 for 86 and steered Essex to victory in the second innings with a score of 67 not out. He invariably did well against Kent.

At the end of the season, while A. O. Jones' side was being mutilated in Australia, he went on a short tour to America where his best knock was an innings of 63 against New York. It was the social side of the game, as much as the game itself, which impressed him in America.

There were (he wrote) banqueting halls, dining rooms, card rooms, racquet and squash courts and on at least one ground, a swimming bath. In Philadelphia, where all these things are to be found, the clubs are run far more on social lines than over here, and special provision is made for lady members.

Such facilities would have had an immediate appeal for Johnny Douglas. He had a zest and an appetite for life which few could emulate. He lived hard and to the full.

He returned to an Essex side where the clouds of doubt again began to gather. The side dropped to eleventh in the Championship table and there was a recurrence of the financial problems that had beset the club a few years earlier, but there was no decline in Douglas' performances. In all

19

matches, he scored 1167 runs and took 83 wickets. His greatest triumph was at Leyton, on Saturday 8 August: in the second innings of the drawn match with Sussex, he scored his maiden century in first-class cricket, 102 not out, having scored 62 in the first innings. On the second day of the game against Kent, three days later, he and Fane put on 207 for the first wicket and Douglas scored his second century in successive innings, 115. This match was also drawn, Hardinge hitting a hundred in each innings.

Earlier in the season, Douglas had bowled Essex to an innings victory over Gloucestershire at Leyton, taking 6 for 45 in the first innings and 6 for 29, bowling unchanged, in the second. In the match against Surrey at the Oval, he had Jack Hobbs caught behind for 99. Two years earlier, he had had the great man lbw for 5, a wicket which prompted Ronald Mason, Hobbs' splendid biographer, to describe Douglas as Hobbs' 'own particular creeping menace'.

The autumn of 1908 was spent in winning the Olympic gold medal in the middleweight boxing tournament, but the euphoria that that triumph evoked could not continue into the following cricket season. McGahey was injured at the beginning of the 1909 season and played for much of the time with a damaged hand. Essex won only two matches, both against Derbyshire, and finished fourteenth in the table with only Derbyshire and Gloucestershire below them. On the playing side, and on the financial side, the county was on a steady downward slide. Times were bad.

Douglas' own form declined somewhat, but he had one moment of triumph. This was the year in which the Australians, under the leadership of M. A. Noble, beat MacLaren's side 2–1 in the Test series and had the better of the two games that were drawn. In Douglas' first encounter with them, at Leyton in May, Essex were beaten by an innings as Bardsley scored 219 and Ransford 174, while Douglas was dismissed for 1 and 18 and took 0 for 125. He

next met them when he played for an England XI at
Blackpool just after the fifth Test in mid-August. He and
A. E. Knight opened the batting and put on 284, which
remains the highest first-wicket partnership against the
Australians in England. Douglas hit his only hundred of the
season, 102. It was somewhat overshadowed later in the
match when Victor Trumper, for whom batting was poetry,
hit 150 in under two hours.

There was some improvement in the form of Essex in
1910. They had five wins and rose to eleventh place in the
Championship table. They beat Kent, the champions, at
Leyton, but Douglas had little part in the victory.

King Edward VII died and the twilight of the age to which
he gave his name set in. At the end of the season, McGahey
resigned as captain of Essex. He was succeeded by John
William Henry Tyler Douglas.

3
Captain Courageous

The cricket world was surprised by the appointment of Douglas as captain of Essex; there were those within the county who were shocked. It has been generally expected that Percy Perrin would succeed Charles McGahey as captain. Perrin was 35, Douglas was 29. Perrin had first played for Essex in 1896, five years before Douglas. He held, and still holds, the record of the highest individual score ever made by an Essex batsman, 343 not out against Derbyshire at Chesterfield in 1904 – a match which, characteristically, Essex lost. He was to gain the reputation of being one of the very finest amateur batsmen never to play for England. He was to become a much respected Test selector. He was well liked by all who knew him and, on McGahey's resignation, it seemed that he would automatically take over. The only disparaging things ever said about Percy Perrin were about his fielding, and he said some of them himself. Legend has it that when asked if he had really stopped one of Hobbs' boundaries down Vauxhall way, he replied reasonably, 'Oh, yes. Mind you, they ran eight.'

That Perrin expected to be captain in succession to McGahey and that he resented being passed over for Douglas is certain, for he declined to play for Essex in the first weeks of Douglas' captaincy. Later, his own generous nature and the wise counsel of others prevailed, and he returned to the

Essex side to become a friend and advisor of the younger man. His humour was always used as a necessary balance when he felt that Johnny was becoming a little too earnest. He is quoted as having deflated one tense situation, when Douglas was rather serious and secretive about the composition of the side for the match which was shortly to start, by enquiring, 'Is Mrs Douglas not playing?'

Whether Perrin ever learned, or guessed, the reason that he was passed over we shall never know. Indeed, there is no record of the reasoning – or politics – that prompted the Essex committee to make its decision to appoint Douglas to the captaincy. We have only conjecture, but it is conjecture which has taken on the ring of historical accuracy over the years.

In his book, *Background of Cricket*, published in 1939, Sir Home Gordon, not one of the most accurate nor one of the most unprejudiced of cricket historians, wrote of Perrin:

> He ought to have led Essex and would have done it admirably. But old Douglas – who succeeded me on my resignation of the first chairmanship of the Club Cricket Conference – held the mortgage on the Leyton Ground and intimated he would foreclose if J.W.H.T. was not made captain.

Sir Home Gordon's general assessment of the Douglases was marked by its acidity, and his book, quite rightly, was severely criticised when it was published, but even his reliance on melodramatic overtones cannot detract completely from his reading of the events that surrounded the appointment of John Douglas to the captaincy of Essex.

Charles Bray, a great friend and admirer of Johnny Douglas, is reluctant to believe the story, but admits, 'John Douglas senior no doubt pulled the strings.' Certainly, old Douglas had become a powerful man. During the winter of

23

1907–8 when the club was threatened with extinction, J. H. Douglas came to the assistance of the committee and took up one of the mortgages on the Leyton Ground. It was for £5000 and the gesture of Douglas senior eased the immediate difficulties and saved the club.

That old Douglas was prone to champion his elder son at every stage of his career is undeniable, and that, as a wealthy man, he was able to influence people is also undeniable. Johnny Douglas himself told the story of how, when he was at Felsted, his father took a side along to play the school for the first time. Old Douglas discovered that his son was being played solely for his bowling and was batting low in the order. He suggested to those in authority that in his opinion his son was a better batsman than a bowler, and from that day, JWHT was moved up the batting order and stayed there. J. H. Douglas was not a man to stand to one side quietly, and his passion was for his son's success. Perhaps, like Forster's Gino, it was a case of 'I continue'.

J. W. H. T. Douglas was to lead Essex for 18 years. No man, save W. G. Grace in Gloucestershire's early days, has led a county for a longer period. No man, save W. G. Grace, has ever commanded with such absolute authority. The demands of captaincy are great. Few captains ever please everybody. In this respect Douglas was no exception. As Charles Bray wrote, there were no half-measures in people's responses to Douglas. 'You either liked and respected John Douglas or you loathed him.' As indicated earlier in this chapter, Sir Home Gordon was one of those who saw no good in Douglas as a captain. In this context, he wrote that John Douglas

. . . would have done himself far more justice as a great cricketer and would really have been a happier man if he had never officially led a county. To meet him away from Essex in other cricket was to find a thoroughly sporting companion. As a skipper of that county he was not only bad but brutal, almost incredible in his ruthlessness. He entirely ruined Hipkin as a player by bullying him.

This is severe judgment, but it is almost a total misconception by one who spent his life on the fringe of first-class cricket, eager to get closer.

Hipkin was a slow left-arm bowler who played for Essex in the 1920s. He was a sportsman of natural talent, also playing professional football as a goalkeeper. There are many who believe that, in an effort to help Hipkin realise his full potential, Douglas stood more from Hipkin, allowed him a licence that he would not grant to others, and that Hipkin was his own worst enemy. Perhaps the incident that best reflects the respective characters of the two men was the one that occurred at Leyton in July 1923.

Essex were playing Middlesex and, facing a total of 489, had lost 6 wickets for 137. Morris and Douglas made a stand and this was followed by a ninth-wicket stand of 160 in 2 hours 10 minutes between Douglas and Franklin which saved the follow-on. Franklin hit his first hundred for Essex and, after 3½ hours faultless batting, Douglas was out for 96. Middlesex were already using their twelfth man in the field when a further indisposition caused them to require the services of Hipkin, the Essex twelfth man. It was Hipkin who caught Douglas. Running along the leg boundary, he took a brilliant catch, one-handed at full stretch. In the professionals' dressing room at close of play, Hipkin was sheepish and morose. He felt that he had really blotted his copy book by catching the old man and went round to the amateurs' dressing room to apologise. Douglas' reply was the one that his friends would have expected: 'You bloody fool, Hipkin. I would have broken your neck if you had missed it.'

Sir Home Gordon quotes another incident in his criticism

of Douglas which concerned Eastman and Nichols. Evidently the two players were injured in a match against Sussex at Hastings and were left by the sea to recuperate. One of them expressed the view to his skipper that he hoped that they would both soon be better and fit to rejoin the county. According to Home Gordon, Douglas' reply was, 'I don't care if you both suffer the pangs of hell while you are unfit to turn out for the county.' What Home Gordon failed to appreciate was that those to whom this remark was made knew their skipper well and would have expected nothing less. Essex was his life.

The two professionals would have also known the kindly side of the man. He had a brusqueness of manner and was, as Pelham Warner described him, a little 'difficile', but his concern for his players has been bettered by none. Charles Bray was sensitive to this quality:

> Yet there was a side of John Douglas which was not shown to any but his intimate friends and sometimes not even to them. A kindliness and understanding of personal problems. He was most generous in helping any professional who got into difficulties financial or otherwise. He regarded them as part of his household.

All the evidence verifies Bray's assessment. When the county arrived for an away fixture Douglas would never think of settling down for the evening before he had visited the professionals in their hotel and checked that they were happy and satisfied with their accommodation. In the morning, before breakfast, he would visit each of the amateurs' rooms and make sure that all was well.

He was a strong disciplinarian, and sometimes an erratic one. He had his likes and his dislikes, and that was one of his failings. He had no time for shirkers or non-triers or for those whom he felt were trying to exploit him. For him every match was important and he treated them all seriously.

Whether the game was a Test match or a friendly match in the Scarborough Festival, Johnny Douglas gave one hundred per cent commitment and expected it from others. In the opinion of G. O. Allen, Douglas would have revelled in the competitive nature of today's cricket, but he would have been totally intolerant of some of today's behaviour on the cricket field.

The brusqueness of his manner and the strength of his discipline hid a kindliness that has already been touched upon. In answer to Home Gordon's attack, R. C. Robertson-Glasgow said simply

> Douglas was said to have been harsh and tyrannical as a captain. This is a misrepresentation of fact. To the slacker and the 'trimmer' he was often merciless. But his wrath was short-lived, and he enjoyed the terse and humorous answer. He was something less than a man who could not stand up to the breeze.

Typical of Douglas is the story of his disciplining of two Essex professionals. They had been involved in some evening antics and were brought before the skipper. In a verbal attack, he reduced them almost to the point of tears and then dismissed them from his presence. As they reached the door, he called to them to return and they slunk back, expecting a continuation of the tirade. 'Silly pair of buggers,' he said, and he slipped a fiver into each of their hands.

There were some, of course, who came off less well. Douglas was always intolerant of A. C. 'Jack' Russell. He considered Russell a player of immense talent who frittered the talent away in riotous living. This was, perhaps, a little harsh, but it is interesting to reflect that one of the anecdotes that Charles Bray tells in his delightful essay on Douglas in *Cricket Heroes* gives credibility to Douglas' opinion of Russell and the substance for it. One of the things that Bray

27

had learned before he played his first game for Essex at Leicester was that the skipper was a stickler for pre-match practice:

> . . . every player, amateur or professional, was not expected but was ordered to appear at pre-match practice each day three-quarters of an hour before the start of play.
>
> It was at Leicester. I was changed and ready even before the skipper. Some of the professionals were already at the nets when we arrived. Douglas immediately told me to go into one net and said to Stan Nichols: 'He's the new boy. I'm sending him in first to slip yourself at him.' I was too busy trying to cope with thunderbolts from Nichols and deliveries almost as difficult from Douglas, to note that Jack Russell was not out at practice. 'Where's Russell?' the skipper asked. 'He's a little tired and stiff, skipper,' replied Jack O'Connor. 'Tired . . . stiff . . . what nonsense!' fumed Johnny. 'Go and tell him that I expect him to be out here within five minutes.'
>
> Jack went off to do his bidding. Russell appeared well within five minutes. He had made a hundred the previous day.

To the young player who showed willingness, dedication and enthusiasm, Johnny Douglas was the most considerate of teachers.

> He had a splendid conception of a captain's duties, and he was a wonderful all-rounder, with a fighting spirit second only, in my experience, to that of Jardine. Douglas was popular with all the men he led, he was a friend to all – he would take an interest in a youngster in the other side just as he would take an interest in a youngster in his own side – and he was brimful of the most sterling qualities.

The writer is Herbert Sutcliffe in his book, *For Yorkshire and England*.

All reports would support Sutcliffe's view. When he learned that I was engaged on this study of Douglas, G. O. Allen went out of his way to make contact and to offer his memories of Douglas. When he was asked why he had gone to such trouble to help, Allen replied simply, 'Because he was so kind to me.'

'Gubby' Allen met Douglas when the great man was captain of England and Allen himself was still at university. Frank Mann brought them together and suggested that Douglas might be able to give Allen some advice as a young quick bowler of great potential. Nothing seemed too much trouble for Douglas as he showed his willingness to help the 20-year-old Allen. He told him about the use of the crease and about swinging the ball and was ever ready to demonstrate. A couple of years later, Allen and others in the Cambridge side were furious with Perrin when, in a match at Colchester, he stood his ground although clearly caught at slip. The umpires felt unable to make a decision and Perrin batted on. The young Allen was most indignant and said a few words to Douglas about how the game was being played. Douglas saw Perrin, and Percy apologised to Allen and said that he had been very much in the wrong. Typically, Douglas felt that the best way that the wounds could be healed quickly was to treat the two parties to dinner.

As an encouragement to an aspiring young bowler, Douglas would place a half-crown on the top of the stumps when he was batting in the nets and it went to the first young bowler who knocked his wicket over. 'Tiny' Waterman remembers the endeavour and enthusiasm that this engendered among young hopefuls. It did not matter to Johnny that a young bowler did not bowl him as long as the youngster kept on trying and never gave up – that was the test. He liked to test people and if they survived, they were accepted.

Charles Bray's debut for Essex was in Douglas' penultimate season. Bray had had a splendid year for Southend Cricket Club and the committee suggested to Douglas that he should be included in the county side for Southend Week, so giving the added attraction of the local champion playing on his own ground.

Douglas dismissed the suggestion contemptuously, saying, 'If he wants to play for the county and you think he's good enough, let him come and play a couple of tough games *after* the festival week.'

The committee apologised to Bray for having raised his hopes and said that they quite understood that Bray would not wish to play in these circumstances. Bray replied that, on the contrary, he would play if Douglas would have him, and he travelled to Leicestershire and Lancashire. After his two matches he left the team at Liverpool, but Douglas took him on one side and said, 'If you care to get in touch with me next April and come down and practise every day, I think I can make something of you. Don't forget.'

Bray did not forget, and before the beginning of the next season he practised assiduously. Douglas put him in the side for the first match of the season and kept him in even though he was not scoring any runs. He went to Douglas and suggested that he be dropped. 'You're trying your hardest, aren't you? Yes! Well, that's all I want from you.' That is all that Douglas wanted of anybody.

His weakness was that he could not always recognise that others were not capable of responding to his 'testing' in the way that he wished. In his delightful study of Percy Fender, Dick Streeton tells of how hurt Fender was by an incident which happened as he set out for Australia on his first tour:

> He was watching the lights of Eastbourne fade in the distance when he was joined on deck by Johnny Douglas. The two men had played with and against each other several times but were still little more than acquaintants. As they

smoked their pipes and talked, Douglas said: 'You know Fender, there is no man in England whose bowling I would rather bat against than yours; and there is no batsman in England I would rather bowl against either.'

From the captain of the side to a young amateur on his first tour, it was a heavy, even insensitive jest. In the context of what we know about Douglas' initial approach to others, it was a testing quip to which he expected a colourful reply, but he had chosen the wrong test for the wrong man, and with it he lost Fender for some years.

In many ways Fender was the antithesis of Douglas. Fender's buoyancy and sense of fun on the field was balanced by a serious and contemplative nature off it. He was a sensitive young man and Douglas' remark wounded him. It caused him to treat Douglas with caution for many years so that the two became polarised, symbolic of different attitudes to the game. In fact, there were great similarities for both were enthusiasts, but Fender had the greater imagination and the cricket played on the Australian tour did nothing to reconcile them.

Tom Pearce tells how, when he became captain of Essex in the early 'thirties, he and Jardine went to toss up at the Oval and declared a 'truce' in the Surrey v. Essex games from the way in which they had been conducted under Fender and Douglas. Evidently it was not unknown for 'Bosser' Martin, the famous groundsman at the Oval, to decide on which strip would be used *after* the captains had tossed and he knew which side was batting first.

In his dealings with Fender, we can see the germ of Douglas' main weakness as a captain, his inability to grasp that others were not as he was himself. Sir Home Gordon was totally accurate when he wrote, 'Johnny felt contempt for any physical weakness or fatigue, being himself as hard as iron and believing everybody could also be if he had grit.'

He was the antithesis of the Duke of Plaza Toro. He led from the front. He led by example. The remark in the *Daily News* that 'he often carried the team on his shoulders' was no more than the truth. Some of the time it was of necessity, at other times it was born of his enthusiasm, his endeavour, his unshaken belief that he would get a wicket next ball.

His own fitness, his ability to bowl for hours on end without loss of accuracy, pace or enthusiasm, caused him to expect the same of others. Although once more Home Gordon tends to hyperbole when he says that George Louden 'dreaded playing as Douglas bowled him thirty overs on end till dead', he is close to the truth. Louden was a fast-medium bowler like Douglas and therefore Douglas expected of him what he was prepared to give, and capable of giving, himself. He could never understand that others might not have the same capabilities, the same endurance.

Often he became so totally submerged in his own efforts to force victory that he lost sight of what was happening elsewhere. A delightful story has been handed down from the late Sir Hubert Ashton concerning his brother, Claude.

In one match, things were not going well for Essex in the field, but John Douglas was bowling with his usual resolution. His problem seemed to be to find someone who could contain things at the other end, so he told Hubert that he was going to give Claude a few overs. Claude Ashton had bowled at university, and in his 18 seasons with the county he took 97 wickets at not too high a cost, but he could never be considered as more than an occasional bowler. Now he bowled several overs of fast-medium and the batsmen, appearing to relish his deliveries, scored freely. Hubert anticipated that his brother would be withdrawn from the attack after four or five overs, but he bowled on and on and the score mounted. At the other end, John Douglas was still pounding away, leaping in excitement, cursing in frustration, as the batsmen played, missed and survived. Claude

Ashton had been bowling for well over an hour before Hubert gathered the courage to approach the skipper and suggest that he remove the younger Ashton from the attack.

'Christ,' said Douglas, 'is he still bowling?'

He was no great tactician as a captain, for he relied entirely on endeavour and inspiration, not imagination nor vision.

He was as stentorian in the field as he was as a referee at the National Sporting Club where his imperative cry of 'Break! Break!' became famous. He attempted to apply the same discipline to his fielders, not always with success. Charles Bray remembers an incident which followed a match in which Essex had dropped very many catches.

Johnny called a team conference and read the riot act. In future for high catches he would shout the name of the player who was to take it and woe betide anyone who disobeyed him. We didn't have any high catches in the next match, but in the following one there was a beauty. Rather belatedly John realized what was expected of him. 'O'Connor!' he yelled. Jack looked aghast, for it wasn't coming anywhere near him. Still he started off. 'No, Nichols!' yelled John. Nick looked just as startled but obediently tucked his head down and ran madly towards the ball. Too late John realized that it was in fact his catch so he made a desperate effort to get to it and might have caught it had not Nichols crashed into him at the crucial moment. 'You bloody fool!' he snarled, 'I'd have caught it, if you hadn't bumped into me.' Then he realized what had happened and roared with laughter.

At other times in the field, his captaincy could be less amusing. In a minor match in which his stepson was playing, the young man misfielded a ball and Johnny held up the game for several minutes while he demonstrated the correct way to field. He and the boy got on well, but after this he felt that cricket was not for him.

'Pickles' was better able to deal with his elder brother. 'Tiny' Waterman recalls a match in which Cecil, amused by his brother's constant and fussy changes in his field placings, went out to field with a pocket filled with small pebbles. He was sent to field in the covers and sure enough, before every over, sometimes before every ball, he was gestured to move one or two paces to right or left. Every time that his brother moved him, Cecil dropped one of his small pebbles on the ground and by the end of the innings he had marked a line about ten yards long which he pointed out to his brother. John saw the joke; he could always see a joke against himself.

He was not always the best judge of a player, but he shares that failing with many great cricketers, and he relied on instinct and on the response to his assessment of a person's willingness and application. This caused him to reject as an Essex prospect Alf Gover, whose endeavours for Surrey were to prove Johnny wrong.

As a captain, John Douglas was brusque, but he was essentially loyal to those under him and they gave him their loyalty, and many of them their love, in return. Nearly 30 years after Johnny Douglas' death, in his charming autobiography, *10 for 66 and All That*, Arthur Mailey was to write:

> Douglas . . . although a strict disciplinarian was an ideal leader, but very often misunderstood and under-rated because his brand of diplomacy was consistent with frankness and moral courage. Another Johnny Douglas now would do cricket no harm.

Perhaps the most accurate assessment of Douglas' qualities of leadership was made by Dudley Carew, probably the most sensitive and eloquent of cricket writers: 'He was not a great captain, but he was most assuredly a great man.'

Those who knew Douglas well would not disagree with that comment.

4
Gentlemen and MCC

It is more than 20 years since the Gentlemen and the Players last took the field in opposition, and indeed, as the distinction between amateur and professional was abolished in 1963, it is possible that the titles 'gentlemen' and 'players' will have little meaning for future generations. Yet there was a time when the matches between the Gentlemen and the Players were the most important events in the domestic cricket calendar.

Between the turn of the century and the outbreak of the first world war there were those followers of cricket who genuinely resented the tours by the Australian and South African sides as detracting from the main business of cricket which was the County Championship. As Denzil Batchelor so aptly commented, 'A fly-by-night success in the unwholesome, torrid atmosphere engendered by those theatrical Test Matches took the minds of all but the most serious off the natural supremacy open to the cricketer: success in Gentlemen v. Players.'

The first meeting was in 1806, and the contests became regular in 1819. The sides would meet three times a year, at Lord's, at the Oval and at the Scarborough or Folkestone Festivals, until the game at the Oval was discontinued in the mid-1930s. Invariably, the matches at Lord's and the Oval were played within a week of each other at the beginning of

July. They were keenly fought, for there was honour to be won and reputations to be made, especially in the contest at Lord's which was the main event of the season.

It was in 1865 at the Oval that W. G. Grace made the first of his 85 appearances for the Gentlemen. He was 16 years old and he stood over six feet. He scored 23 and 12 not out and had match figures of 7 for 125. He was to dominate the matches between the Gentlemen and the Players for the next 40 years until, on 18 July 1906, his fifty-eighth birthday, he scored 74 before being caught by Albert Trott off the bowling of Jayes. As he left the wicket, having played his last innings for the Gentlemen, the Oval echoed to applause, mighty and emotional, for the gods of cricket are not often among us.

When the sides met again, at Scarborough in September, only M. W. Payne and C. G. Napier remained from the Gentlemen's team which had drawn at the Oval. Batting at no. 7, the place which had been occupied by W. G. Grace in his last game, was John Douglas. He was then 24 years old and it was the first of the 30 appearances he was to make for the Gentlemen over the next 21 years. In those 30 matches, he was to take a total of 90 wickets. Only W. G. Grace, with 271, bettered that total for the Gentlemen.

Douglas' first match was eminently satisfactory. He took the wickets of both openers, Hayward and Rhodes, and Myers in the first innings at a cost of 89 runs; in the second innings he dismissed Rhodes and J. T. Tyldesley for 70 runs. He scored 10 and 35 not out, and the match was drawn.

The following season, 1907, he met with no success at Lord's, but a week later at the Oval, he had a magnificent game, sending back Hobbs, Hayward, Braund, Tarrant and Trott in the first innings at a cost of 94 runs and scoring 31 and 33. It was the first time that he dismissed Hobbs in these matches and Hobbs was always to insist that Douglas was probably the most difficult bowler he faced, with his outswinger being particularly awkward. Over the next three years he scored few runs and took few wickets until, in September 1910 at Scarborough, he took 4 for 79 and 4 for 68.

In 1911, he had become captain of Essex and enjoyed a fine season. In all matches he scored 1279 runs, his highest aggregate to date, at an average of 29.74, and took 82 wickets. Against Nottinghamshire at Trent Bridge, he passed the 150 mark for the first time when he scored 176 in 5¾ hours as he and Perrin, who scored a hundred in each innings, put on 221 for the second wicket. On only six other occasions that season did he reach 50, but one of them was for the Gentlemen against the Players at Lord's.

The match at the Oval which was played on 6, 7 and 8 July was treated as a Test trial, but Douglas had little success, 0 and 14 not out, 1 for 44 and 0 for 6. The players went straight from the Oval to Lord's, where they played on 10, 11 and 12 July. 'Plum' Warner considered that the two sides that were fielded in this match were probably the strongest ever put out. Looking at the names on the scorecard, one cannot disagree with Warner's verdict. C. B. Fry captained the Gentlemen and he had in his side Spooner, Warner, Jessop, F. R. Foster, Day, Le Couteur, Campbell, Burns, Gibson and Douglas. Playing in these matches for the last time, Tom Hayward captained a Players' side which included Hobbs, J. T. Tyldesley, Rhodes, Hirst, Tarrant and Barnes.

From the start of the match, the wicket gave the bowlers some assistance and Spooner and Campbell fell to the great Sydney Barnes with only 26 scored. Warner then joined Fry in a stand of 82, both batsmen scoring fifties. It was the batting of Douglas, however, which won the accolades. Stern and steady, he withstood the wiles of Barnes and scored 72. It was an invaluable innings and held the side together when Barnes, who had dismissed Warner, threatened to run through them.

While Barnes was being rested, too long according to Warner, although he did send down 34 overs, Foster launched an attack on the bowling of Rhodes and the Gentlemen reached a very respectable total of 352. Douglas batted 3¼ hours for his 72 and not for the first time, nor for the last, he was accused of over-caution, but *Wisden* considered that he had never played better and that his resolution on a doubtful wicket had made the remarkably large total possible.

On the second day, according to *Wisden*, 'the Gentlemen showed tremendous form all round, and outplayed their opponents at every point. The wicket was never really good, the ball constantly doing unexpected things.' It is significant of the times, however, that at lunchtime on this erratic wicket, the Players' score stood at 150 for 4. After lunch, Douglas and Foster took the remaining six wickets in an hour while 51 runs were scored. They 'came off the ground very fast, the rather fiery wicket suiting them to a nicety.' Douglas bowled Hayward, Tarrant and Iremonger, caught and bowled Buckenham, and had Hardinge taken by Burns. His five wickets cost him 53 runs and he bowled 19.1 overs. It was the only occasion during the season when he took five wickets in an innings.

Fry and Spooner batted magnificently in an opening stand of 122 in the second innings so that the Gentlemen were in sight of victory. Fry declared on the third morning after batting on for under an hour. Douglas had again distinguished himself, scoring 22 not out. The Players needed 423 in 4 hours 50 minutes. At lunch, they had scored 95 for the loss of Tom Hayward. 77 runs were scored in 40 minutes for the second wicket and 57 runs in 35 minutes for the third wicket. Hobbs, missed at short leg by Campbell when 94, played one of his very great innings and scored 154 not out. He was most troubled by Douglas' away-swinger and had some luck not to be caught in the slips, but nothing could detract from the magnificence of his achievement to play so finely on such a poor wicket. He made his runs in 3¼ hours, his innings, according to *Wisden*, 'being incomparably his best during the whole season'.

Douglas took the last two wickets of the match and the Gentlemen won a splendid game by 130 runs. It was the first time that Douglas had played on a winning side for the Gentlemen for he had not been in the team at the Oval in 1908 when they had last beaten the Players. *Wisden*'s epitaph on the match was significant: 'Scoring 72 and not out 22, and taking in all seven wickets for 91 runs, Douglas played a great part in the Gentlemen's victory.'

A fortnight to three weeks before this match at Lord's, MCC had begun to select the side to visit Australia the following winter. The team was to leave England at the end of September. At first, eight men were invited – C. B. Fry, who was to captain the side, R. H. Spooner, Pelham Warner, F. R. Foster, S. F. Barnes, Jack Hobbs, Wilfred Rhodes and Herbert Strudwick – but Spooner was unable to accept the invitation to tour, while Fry, having felt at first that he would be able to make the trip, gave no definite reply to the committee.

It is not now generally realised that however much the Golden Age was dominated by amateurs, those amateurs could not give all their time to cricket; business, finance and other interests did not allow them to. Reggie Spooner, whose grace and handsome style was so brilliantly evoked by Sir Neville Cardus, played in only ten Test matches in the whole of his career, which lasted for 24 years. The average Test player today has usually played that many by the end of his first year in international cricket, and there was nothing 'average' about Reggie Spooner. Charles Fry was able to play in only a third of the Test matches for which he was chosen during his heyday, much of his time being given to his work with the Training Ship *Mercury*.

By the end of July 1911, Warner, Foster, Barnes, Hobbs, Rhodes and Strudwick had accepted the invitation to go to Australia the following winter and, after his success for the Gentlemen against the Players at Lord's, an invitation was sent to J. W. H. T. Douglas. He readily accepted. He was in the enviable position of never having to refuse such an invitation for he had a father eager for his success and wealthy enough to make it possible for his son to pursue his sporting activities.

A few days after Douglas had accepted the invitation to join the side, Kinneir, Iremonger and 'Tiger' Smith were also asked to tour. At the beginning of August, the committee realised that the side was weak in slip-fielding and invited Woolley and Mead to come along as well as George Gunn. Woolley and Mead had the added advantage of being rather useful left-handed batsmen, and at that time, Woolley was also a fine bowler.

In mid-August, Fry announced that he would not be able to captain the side and Warner was invited to take over. Since the selection of the first eight men in June, the committee, under the leadership of Lord Harris, had made no invitations unless their selections were approved by Fry and Warner. The others mainly responsible for selecting the side were Lord Hawke and J. R. Mason, although it must be realised that selection committees were of a more nebulous nature than they are today.

Like Fry and Spooner, Gilbert Jessop was forced to decline the invitation and Hitch, Vine and Hearne completed the side. The selection of 'Young' Jack Hearne was not finalised until 14 September, the Middlesex committee having at first opposed his making the tour on the grounds that he was too young and the tour would be too arduous.

Warner was well pleased with the side in his charge for he felt that never before had such great care and deliberation been taken in selecting a team to tour Australia. He felt that the Test trials had helped greatly, but the editor of *Wisden* and Jack Hobbs could not agree with him on this point.

The team that finally set out was P. F. Warner (Middlesex – captain), J. W. H. T. Douglas (Essex), F. R. Foster, Kinneir and Smith (Warwickshire), Hobbs, Strudwick and Hitch (Surrey), Rhodes (Yorkshire), Iremonger and George Gunn (Nottinghamshire), Mead (Hampshire), Woolley (Kent), Vine (Sussex), Barnes (Staffordshire) and J. W. Hearne (Middlesex). Warner, Rhodes, Barnes, Hobbs, Gunn and Strudwick had toured Australia before and there were many who thought that ten players inexperienced in Australian conditions was too large a number. But looked at with the advantage of historical perspective, it was a formidable side. Of the first eight batsmen in the order, only Douglas and Foster were to fail to reach 35,000 runs before their careers ended.

Perhaps the most remarkable thing about the side was that it contained only three amateurs and, since Warner had ascended to the captaincy, no-one had been designated as vice-captain. Warner had been captain of Middlesex since 1908 and was also rich in experience in leading MCC sides, but both Douglas and Foster had only become captains of their counties in 1911, the year of their selection.

Under Douglas, Essex had made considerable improvement and risen to sixth in the table. They might have done even better had the bowling not rested so heavily on Buckenham and Douglas himself. The captain was quite aware of their need for, in an interview the year before, he had stated, 'Our great need just now is a slow left-handed bowler.' Douglas led by example, as he was to do for the next 18 seasons, and Warner wrote of him: 'In all his cricket he was untiring, the hot weather having no effect on his energy.' When he set sail for Australia he was 29 years old.

Frank Foster was only 22 when the team set out and, like Douglas, he had captained his county for one season. The year before he took over, Warwickshire had finished four-teenth in the table. Under his leadership they won the Championship for the first time in their history. A fast-medium left-arm bowler and a hard-hitting unorthodox right-handed batsman, Foster did the double in county matches alone in 1911 and it was no surprise that he was one of *Wisden*'s 'Five Cricketers of the Year' in the annual which covered that season. He was a fine slip-fielder and a thinker on the game. He was to lead Warwickshire with distinction and inspiration until the first world war, when his career was ended by a motor-cycle accident.

Should anything happen to Warner, it was one of these two men that would have to take over. It was surprising that no vice-captain was appointed in advance for, on the last MCC tour to Australia, F. L. Fane had had to take over when A. O. Jones was in hospital, and on the tour to South Africa in 1909–10, Fane had again shared the leadership, this time with Leveson-Gower.

These considerations had no place in people's minds when the team set off from St Pancras on the morning of Friday 29 September 1911. It was a festive occasion, a farewell for a small group of warriors setting out for a far land in an effort to recapture the mythical Ashes. Crowds gathered inside and outside the station more than an hour before the team was due to leave. The platform was a dense mass of well-wishers, and all the dignitaries of cricket had gathered there: Lord Harris, Lord Hawke, Fry, Stoddart, C. E. Green, whose administration had done much to keep Essex alive and who was a director of the Orient Line on one of whose ships the team was to sail, Faulkner, J. R. Mason, Spooner, C. I. Thornton, Leveson-Gower, Perrin, McGahey, 'Razor' Smith, Gerry Weigall, Colin Blythe, Tom Richardson were among those clustered to say 'good luck'. So, too, was J. H. Douglas, happy and proud for his son.

Lord Harris invited the team into the waiting room where

they drank a 'stirrup cup' with him and he made a short speech. He said that MCC was convinced that it was sending to Australia one of the best teams that had left England and that 'it possessed brilliancy and soundness in batting; there was a variety of bowling for every species of wicket.' As the train left the station the crowds chanted 'Bring back the Ashes'. At Tilbury, there were more speeches, the principal one by C. E. Green who acted as host, and Warner replied, touched by the affection that had been shown to the side.

To avoid the Bay of Biscay, Hobbs and Strudwick travelled overland and joined the ship at Marseilles, but the rest of the party left Tilbury on a fine autumn evening in late September. The liner *Orvieto* took its valuable cargo of cricketers on the eighteenth English tour of Australia. Among those cricketers was J. W. H. T. Douglas, eager in anticipation of an opportunity to play for England for the first time, but totally unaware of what fate had in store for him.

5
Captain of England

This was the age, of course, when journeys to Australia were leisurely and there was time for social relaxation. The whole voyage to Adelaide took just over five weeks, and there were stops at Gibraltar, Marseilles, Naples, Taranto, Port Said and Colombo. At Colombo, the team played a game against Ceylon whom they bowled out for 59. It was the first time an English side had played in what is now Sri Lanka for 18 years. Douglas batted at no. 9 and scored 14 not out. He did not bowl.

The party arrived in Adelaide to the customary welcome and within a week Warner and Tom Pawley, the manager, met with Clem Hill to thrash out the arrangements and conditions of play, something which Warner felt, rightly, should have been done long before the tour had begun.

The opening match of the tour was against South Australia at Adelaide, and began on 10 November. Warner won the toss and MCC ran up a huge score of 563. Warner himself, batting at no. 4, was in splendid form and hit 151. Gunn hit 106 and Foster a fierce 158. Douglas, at no. 7 (Woolley was no. 8) made 10.

Barnes and Foster opened the MCC bowling and Foster bowled Mayne in his second over. Stirling was run out by Hobbs for 1 and S. Hill bowled by Barnes for 0 before Clem Hill and J. N. Crawford effected a mild recovery. Douglas was brought on as first change and his bowling career in Australia started disastrously. He was no-balled four times in his first four deliveries. In his eagerness, that bounding run was taking him over the crease. The umpire indicated the problem and Douglas finished the over without further mishap. Warner immediately changed him to the other end so that he would bowl into the wind and he settled into his usual rhythm, containing both Hill and Crawford but not taking a wicket.

South Australia were dismissed for 141 on the third day (Foster 4 for 58, Barnes 3 for 38) and followed on after lunch. This time Douglas and Foster opened the bowling against Clem Hill and Down. Each bowler took a wicket in his first over. Douglas' first wicket was the great Clem Hill, the Australian captain. Warner was in ecstasies about the delivery: 'The ball which beat Clem Hill swerved into the batsman – that is, from his off stump on to his middle and leg – and came like lightning off the pitch. Hill was so late for it, that he looked to have a hole in his bat.'

Douglas' bowling was the feature of the innings. He bowled S. Hill, Webster and Whitty as well as Clem Hill, and Blackman was stumped off him by Strudwick, for these were the days when wicket-keepers stood up to bowlers of Douglas' fast-medium pace. He finished with 5 for 65 and South Australia were bowled out on the final day for 228, giving MCC a comforting start to the tour with victory by an innings and 194 runs.

The sense of elation was short-lived, however. Warner had been feeling very ill on the voyage out. After he had reached 80 in his innings against South Australia, and at the close of play on the first day, when he was 112, he felt 'quite done up'. The next morning he felt perfectly well and continued his innings until, on 151, he pulled a long hop into his own stumps. He led the team in the field without problems and, naturally, was delighted at the manner of its victory.

The team left Adelaide for Melbourne on the afternoon of Tuesday 14 November, and that night Warner was taken ill. He had played his one and only innings in Australia, being well enough to end his convalescence only at the very end of the tour. He was told later by the doctors that he had run the very gravest risks in having played at Colombo and Adelaide.

The immediate question for Warner to answer at the moment he was stricken down was who would now lead the side. Warner outlined the events and his reasoning in his *England v. Australia 1912*, which is based on the reports he sent to the *Westminster Gazette*.

> The MCC had done me high honour in appointing me captain and selector – a sort of dictator, in fact! When the question of a vice-captain came up before the Committee, it was agreed to leave that entirely to me, and as regards a selection committee the feeling was that if I was in any doubt as to the actually strongest side I would naturally consult Rhodes and others who had previous experience of tours in Australia. When I fell ill I had to consider whether Douglas or Foster should act as vice-captain. Both were county captains of the same standing, both having been appointed to their positions at the beginning of the summer of 1911. Foster had a particularly good record, having in his first season led Warwickshire to the top of the tree, but Douglas had done well with Essex, and was senior both in age and in cricketing experience, having played for Essex long before Foster appeared for Warwickshire, and having represented the Gentlemen against the Players at Lord's as far back as 1907.
>
> It would have been unfair, then, to have passed over Douglas, and my choice, therefore, fell on him.

Warner was confined to his room, and in fact he was not able to go to a match and see a ball bowled until the fourth Test but, as Jack Hobbs states, he retained authority in matters concerning the tour.

The party was now down to 15 players and Douglas had five matches in which to lead the side before the first Test and to iron out any problems. The first match under his captaincy was highly successful from his point of view, a win over Victoria by 49 runs, his own contribution being 4 for 41 and 4 for 37, and 33 not out and 5 not out. Foster hit another century and Hitch bowled well. Hobbs hit 88 and Rhodes 66, but the Australian press and public were not impressed and the opinion was expressed that England would not win a Test in the forthcoming series.

The first game with New South Wales was ruined by the weather. Douglas was lbw to the leg-spinner Hordern for 0, but he took 3 for 35 before rain brought an early close to the match. There followed ten days in Queensland, with victories over the State side and over Toowoomba in a non-first-class match, and a drawn game with an Australian XI.

The Australian XI consisted of six of the Queensland side and the leading players from other states, Armstrong of Victoria, Crawford of South Australia, and Trumper, Kelleway and Minnett of New South Wales. Douglas won the toss, but Rhodes, Vine and Mead were out for 'ducks' and Foster made only 9 so that 4 wickets were down for 21 runs. Douglas then joined Kinneir in a stand of 94. Kinneir perished on the square-leg boundary, but Douglas battled on. At the end of the first day he was 89 not out, and he reached his hundred just before MCC were bowled out on the second morning. He batted for over 4½ hours, but it was an innings of determination when faced with adversity, the situation which always brought the best out of him and for which his defensive qualities were most admirably suited.

The game was restricted to three days so that there was never much hope of a result. Crawford scored a century, Barnes took five wickets and when MCC batted again Hearne, who had a lean tour, scored 89 not out.

Surprisingly, although the Australian XI scored 347 and Douglas used six bowlers, he did not bowl himself.

The team now moved back to Sydney for the first Test match which began on Friday 15 December 1911. It was John Douglas' first Test match and he was captain of England.

Hitch had broken down and so joined Warner on the sidelines. Strudwick was given the wicket-keeping spot in preference to Smith. Iremonger and Vine had done little to warrant selection so places were found for Mead and Hearne. Gunn had a damaged hand, but he played. Clem Hill won the toss and Bardsley and Kelleway opened for Australia on a good wicket. Foster opened with the wind behind him to give added venom to his fast swerving ball. It was expected that Barnes would, as a matter of course, take the ball at the other end, but it was Douglas who opened the bowling with Foster. It was a decision that was to reverberate down the years and was to come close to costing Douglas the England captaincy after only one match.

There is consistency in the reports of those who were on the field. Douglas, in his enthusiasm, told Barnes that he was just going to try a couple of overs himself with the new ball. Barnes had no option but to defer to his skipper, although in some colourful language he queried what he was doing on the field if he was not going to open the bowling.

As Douglas bowled only four overs before handing the ball to Barnes, it is difficult for the modern reader to understand what all the fuss was about. Barnes himself, who had a great admiration for Douglas, 'so fine a sportsman', was quoted years after as saying that 'It is generally agreed that, but for misjudgment on his part, we should not have lost the first Test.' Warner, who saw nothing of the match and wrote his account of it from the reports given him by the players, said, with reference to Douglas, 'He was guilty of a tactical error in not starting with Barnes. One should not use the best bowler in the world as a change-bowler.' The point was that Douglas, Foster and Barnes all had a right to feel that they should use the new ball, but Douglas would have bowled his very best whenever he bowled. Barnes was a different character, a fiery and temperamental man who felt he had been slighted in not being given the new ball, a feeling which affected his performance when he was asked to bowl.

For Douglas little went right. He took his first Test wicket when he had Bardsley caught behind, but Trumper scored 113 and Australia reached 447. The leg-spin and googlies of Hordern troubled England, who finished 129 behind on the first innings. Douglas was one of Hordern's five victims, for 0.

When Australia batted again Douglas took 4 for 50, Kelleway and Hordern bowled, Cotter lbw and Trumper caught and bowled. England were left needing 438 to win, a task which they found well beyond them, and they lost by 146 runs. Douglas hit his first runs in Test cricket, 32, before falling to Hordern again.

After the match the general feeling was that, without Warner to lead them, England would lose every Test. Warner's criticism of Douglas was that by the time of the first Test 'he did not have the side in hand.' This was the assessment in several of his books, always using the same words. In his review of the tour for the *Westminster Gazette*, which was also used as *Wisden*'s review of the tour, he clarified this statement.

> . . . at first he did not fulfil expectations. He did not have his side in hand by the time the first Test match was reached, not having any fixed idea as to who were his best batsmen and bowlers, nor were the fielders always in the places to which they are accustomed. The side was somewhat "ragged" to look at, and this should not have been so, for between my falling ill and the first Test match he had command of the side in the field for five matches, time enough to have evolved a more or less definite plan of attack and defence.

When news reached Warner that complaints were being made about Douglas' methods of procedure he sent for the senior members of the side and discussed the question of allowing Douglas to continue as captain. Jack Hobbs was one of those called to this council of war and, as he stated later, he took the view that a change of captaincy would produce friction and much unpleasantness. It was decided that Douglas should continue as captain, but the decision was not unanimous.

The first Test match had finished on 21 December and the second Test began on 30 December. The match that separated them was at Bendigo against fifteen of the local side. This was scant opportunity to regroup scattered forces, but there was much talking, much deliberation and, as Warner was quick to point out afterwards, Douglas was ever ready to listen to advice. He had bowled splendidly in the second innings of the first Test, but he had not fielded well (it was said that he should have run out Cotter first ball) and, most importantly, his field-placings were considered poor. There was much to discuss.

Although his stock as a captain was low, Douglas' reputation as a man and as a personality was growing. His response to the address of welcome at the Town Hall in Melbourne had been one of the shortest but most famous speeches ever made by a captain of MCC: 'I hate speeches. As Bob Fitzsimmons once said, "I ain't no blooming orator, but I'll fight any man in this blinking country." '

It was in Melbourne, too, in the match against Victoria, that an anonymous wag in the crowd had dubbed him 'Johnny Won't Hit Today' when he was in the middle of one of his most dour efforts with the bat, having moved into one of those states when he became totally becalmed. The nickname stuck, and little that Douglas did with the bat over the next 17 years was calculated to rid him of this title. In truth, he was rather proud of it.

England made two changes for the second Test match, Hitch and Smith taking the places of Kinneir and Strudwick. Australia fielded an unchanged side. Both Hitch and 'Tiger' Smith were making their Test debuts, and the selection of Smith surprised many, for Strudwick was considered to be the first choice 'keeper and he had not kept badly at Sydney. For his chance to play in a Test match, Smith remained eminently grateful to Douglas. Nearly 70 years later, when dictating his autobiography to Pat Murphy, he recalled:

> Looking back on it now, I suppose it was a stroke of good fortune for me that Warner was taken ill after the first match. I was well aware that he thought highly of Herbert Strudwick and I had no doubts that he'd keep in the Tests. But the replacement captain, Johnny Douglas, was a different type: where Warner always wanted the pros to look up to him and to let them realize he was the boss, Johnny was as straight as a gunbarrel. There was none of this 'Mr Douglas' nonsense with him. He let you know where you stood with him. He was one of us, more of a professional amateur than an amateur of the old school. We all respected him greatly for his strong qualities and his honesty, and the success of that tour owed a lot to Johnny Douglas.
>
> It was Johnny who decided I'd play in the second Test because Strudwick had been given his chance in the first Test and he wanted to be fair to us both.

Apart from its personal comments on Douglas' character, Smith's observation is interesting in that it credits Douglas with a strong influence in team selection when most people believed that Warner still held the reins firmly. Warner's own explanation of the selection was that Strudwick had kept splendidly at Sydney, but whenever he had played Smith had shown fine form, and after due consideration it was decided to give him his first opportunity of distinguishing himself for England against Australia.

Smith learned of his selection on Christmas Day and he said that, in spite of the defeat at Sydney and the adverse comments made about the side in the press, team spirit was very high. Within half an hour of the start of the second Test match it must have been even higher.

Australia won the toss and Foster bowled the first over, a maiden, to Kelleway. It is most probable that, following the reaction to his opening the bowling himself at Sydney, Douglas intended giving the ball to Barnes in this match, but Smith throws an amusing light on the question. The last ball of Foster's over went through to Smith, who instinctively threw the ball to Barnes. 'It was just a natural thing on my part,' he says. 'Well, Barney needed no second bidding and he was off to the railway end like a shot to pace out his run-up. Johnny Douglas joined him swiftly and after a long chat, Barney got his way and the rest is history.' It is interesting to reflect that had Smith not thrown the ball to Barnes, the whole course of the tour and Douglas' place in cricket history may have been different.

Barnes had been feeling unwell a few days before the game and had been running a temperature high enough for a doctor to consider it doubtful that he would be fit for the Test. He felt weak on the morning of the game, but was quoted later as saying that he had a curious feeling that it would be his day and that when he got the ball in his hands he felt he could do anything with it.

The first ball he bowled hit Bardsley on the toe and went on to break the wicket. If he had not been bowled, he would have been lbw. Kelleway went next ball. He stepped in front of his wicket and played no shot at a ball which he believed was going down the leg-side, but it moved back at him and he was lbw. The over was described by Clem Hill, the Australian skipper, as being the most torrid he ever witnessed. The first two deliveries had accounted for Bardsley and Kelleway and the left-handed Hill came in to save the side. He received an off-break, then an inswinger. He played no stroke at the fifth ball of the over, which was an away-swinger, and the last ball was pitched on his leg stump and knocked back his off stump.

Warwick Armstrong went back to what was Barnes' quick leg-break and the ball touched the outside edge to give Smith his first dismissal in Test cricket. A shower of rain gave Australia some respite, but at lunch they were 32 for 4. Barnes had taken four wickets for three runs in nine overs. It is considered by most judges to have been the greatest spell of opening bowling in the history of England v. Australia Test matches. He took his four wickets before he conceded a run, which came when Trumper snicked a ball through Douglas' legs at slip.

Incredibly, in the midst of this success, Barnes had begun to feel unwell again. His head was spinning and he had to plead with Douglas to be taken off as he could hardly see the other end of the wicket. One can understand Douglas' reluctance to remove his ace bowler from the attack, but he was rested until after lunch when he had Minnett dropped on 0 and then caught by Hobbs so that he finished with 5 for 44 in 23 overs. Foster bowled Trumper, always a prize scalp, and Hitch had Ransford caught behind. Douglas removed Carter in the same way and Woolley bowled Whitty with the one ball he delivered. Rhodes, incidentally, bowled only two overs in the match, in the second innings, and he did not take a first-class wicket on the entire tour.

Australia were dismissed for 184. England lost Hobbs for 6 before the close of play, but Rhodes and Hearne batted well. Hearne handled the leg-spin of Hordern, the Australian demon bowler, with confidence and composure, but after Hearne's fall, caught behind off Cotter, England collapsed. Hordern took the last four wickets, including Douglas, bowled, and they were out for a disappointing

265. It was not quite the start to the New Year that England had hoped for.

On the third day, Australia reached 267 for 8, and they added only another 32 runs on the fourth morning. Bardsley was run out and the remaining nine wickets were taken by Foster and Barnes. Warwick Armstrong's 90 was the backbone of the Australian innings. Foster sent down 38 overs and took 6 for 91. He was for many the best bowler of his type that they had ever seen, and his career was all too brief.

England needed 219 to win. Rhodes and Hobbs put on 57 for the first wicket before Gunn joined Hobbs in a stand which dominated the Australian bowling and ended the threat of Hordern. Gunn was caught behind at 169, but Hearne and Hobbs saw England to victory before the end of the day. Hobbs hit a brilliant 126 not out and silenced the Australian critics who felt that he was destined for a bad tour. Although he had had little personal success, Douglas had won his first Test match and there was joy in the England camp.

Once more only a minor match separated the Test matches. At Geelong, MCC took on fifteen of the local side as they had done at Bendigo. Douglas scored 43 and did not bowl.

For the third time Hill won the toss and Australia batted. The Adelaide wicket for the third Test was every bit as good as the wicket at Melbourne had been a week earlier, but the Australian rout was even more complete. It was Barnes and Foster again who did the damage. Foster, bowling a type of leg-theory, took 5 for 36, and Barnes had 3 for 71. Douglas bowled 7 overs and took the wicket of Carter, the last man, for 7 runs. Australia were all out for 133 an hour before the close. Hobbs and Rhodes reached 49 that evening and put England on the road to victory. They took their stand to 147 the next day and Hobbs went on to make 187. Foster made 71, Douglas 35, and England reached 501.

Australia fought back well for 476, Clem Hill making 98 and Carter 72. Warner felt that Douglas bowled Hearne too much (his ten overs cost 61 runs) and himself and Barnes too little. Douglas bowled Kelleway and Armstrong at a cost of 71 runs and Barnes' figures were 46.4 overs, 7 maidens, 5 wickets for 105 runs, which hardly suggests that he was underbowled.

England needed only 109 to win, a task that they accomplished with ease, and the whole complexion of the tour had now changed. On the eve of the second Test, England were considered to have no chance in the series. Since then their bowlers had twice destroyed Australia and they led 2–1 in the Tests. The team was buoyant and Douglas' reputation had grown. He neither batted nor bowled against the fifteen of Ballarat and he took his only rest of the tour when the team went to Tasmania. While MCC won their matches with the islanders by eight wickets and by an innings, Douglas holidayed on a hunting and fishing expedition near Launceston. There was no sport he did not enjoy and he strove to be proficient at all.

In the second match in Tasmania, the one at Hobart, Frank Woolley scored 305 not out. He batted no. 3 and in his book, *The King of Games*, he tells a story which throws some light on the firm control that Douglas had on the side. Woolley complains that in Australia he invariably batted no. 8 or no. 9 and as he was in the side for his batting, he could not understand the reasons for this. He was down to bat at no. 9 in Hobart, but Barnes told him to get his pads on when the openers went in as he felt that Mead might be 'missing' when a wicket fell.

When Kinneir was out, Woolley hustled out without daring to look at his captain's face. He adds, 'I must say here that Mr Douglas, who captained during Mr Warner's illness, did not cross over to Tasmania with us so Mr F. R. Foster was captain.' Woolley's facts, or his ghost's, are not quite right, for Douglas was in Tasmania sporting in other ways, but Woolley's implication is clear: he would not have got away with promoting himself in the batting order had Douglas been captain. One doubts whether he would even have tried it.

Woolley was at no. 6 in the match against Victoria which preceded the fourth Test. This match was played for Blackham's benefit, but the excessive heat kept the attendance down. Hearne played a fine innings of 143, but it turned out to be his last real contribution of the tour. Douglas batted for 5½ hours and scored 140.

Even in the hottest weather he wore no headgear, and the legend grew of him that he was immune to sun-stroke. Bronzed, his mass of black hair always parted meticulously in the centre and never untidy, he stood 5 feet 10 inches and was powerfully built with shoulders and arms of immense strength. When bowling, he rubbed the ball constantly on his bare forearm to maintain the shine. This habit led to the assessment that he had skin of unusual toughness. A square jaw and a firm straight mouth accentuated regular, classical features, and piercing blue eyes looked out from beneath shaggy eyebrows. It was a face of strength, sensitivity and an awareness of distinction. That it was never surmounted by a cap, even in temperatures of 108 degrees as on the first day of the game with Victoria when a bright sun blazed out of a clear sky, was part of Douglas' contest with the elements, for it was against the elements as well as his opponents that he measured his strength. It must be remembered, too, that his first century of the tour had been scored in the intense heat of Brisbane.

MCC had been 125 for 5 when Douglas joined Hearne. Hobbs, Rhodes, Gunn, Mead and Woolley were out and all, according to Warner, appeared 'exhausted by their efforts, drinks being frequently brought out to refresh both batsmen and fielders'. Douglas, on the other hand, 'seemed

1. The picture of J. W. H. T. Douglas which hangs in the clubhouse at Wanstead CC. He played for the club and he and his father did much to help them.

2. Olympic middleweight boxing champion: London, October 1908.

3. The three amateurs of the 1911–12 tour: Foster, Douglas and Warner.

4. The tie-clip presented to Douglas from an unknown source in recognition of his captaincy of the Ashes-winning England team in 1911–12.

5. The MCC side to South Africa, 1913–14. *Standing:* A. E. Relf, H. Strudwick, I. D. Difford (manager), M. W. Booth, P. Mead, S. F. Barnes, F. E. Woolley. *Seated:* J. B. Hobbs, M. C. Bird, J. W. H. T. Douglas, Hon. I. H. Tennyson, W. Rhodes. *On ground:* E. J. Smith, J. W. Hearne.

6. Douglas posing in the nets.

7. Warwick Armstrong's great Australian side of 1921, the undoing of John Douglas. *Standing:* W. Bardsley, J. S. Ryder, H. L. Hendry, J. M. Gregory, E. R. Mayne, T. J. E. Andrews, Sydney Smith (manager). *Seated:* A. A. Mailey E. A. McDonald, H. L. Collins, W. W. Armstrong, C. G. Macartney, H. Carter, J. M. Taylor. *On ground:* C. E. Pellew, W. A. Oldfield.

Practising before the start of
the first Test, 1921.

Armstrong and Douglas.
The ruthless efficiency, tactical
and technical, of the Australians
took cricket into a new era and
effectively ended Douglas'
career as England's captain.

10.   England take the field in 1921, led by Douglas.

11.   Douglas goes out to bat at Leeds in the third Test, 1921.

12.   The Australians leave Waterloo at the end of their 1921 tour. Douglas senior, with bowler hat and moustache, is in sombre mood in the centre of the picture.

13.   Soccer for charity at Bognor in 1925. *Left to right:* F. W. Gilligan, A. E. R. Gilligan, Johnny Douglas, Harold Gilligan and Maurice Tate.

14. The bounding action, the unflinching endeavour.

to enjoy thoroughly the exhausting conditions' although *Wisden* suggested that his slowness in the fifth hour of his innings was because the heat was taking its toll of him. He and Hearne added 214 for the sixth wicket and MCC went on to win by eight wickets, Douglas taking 2 for 52 in the Victorian second innings.

The Australian cause in their efforts to draw level in the series was not helped by the rift that seemed to have developed between the Board of Control, which was a newly formed body, and the players, and the general state of Australian cricket was unhealthy. Their chances of survival were not improved in the fourth Test when Douglas won the toss for the first time in the series and asked Australia to bat. There had been rain in Melbourne and Barnes, Rhodes, Foster and Warner, as well as Douglas, had looked at the wicket and decided that it was damp enough to cause problems for whichever side batted first. They had read the wicket well. Australia were bowled out by Barnes and Foster for 191 on the opening day and Douglas did not need to use himself. Hobbs and Rhodes then opened with their record 323 and the Ashes were within England's grasp. Douglas had the disappointment of scoring 0, falling again to a leg-spinner, Armstrong, but England made 589 and the future looked bleak for Australia as they began the fourth day 398 runs in arrears.

This was to be Douglas' day. He was ever one to grasp the moment of challenge and here was his opportunity to finish in triumph, to complete the recovery that had started after that disaster of the first Test. He brought himself quickly into the attack and bowled off a longer run than usual. Bounding in with his easy rhythm and fluent delivery, he moved the ball in the air and seemingly achieved that increase of pace off the pitch which the scientists deny, but which the batsman still believes to be a reality. His length was relentlessly accurate and the batsmen were entirely on the defensive.

Armstrong and Minnett were bowled by fierce break-backs. Hill was beaten by pace when he attempted to pull. Hordern and Carter were caught. At one point, the England skipper sent down 15 overs from which only 21 runs were scored while he took 4 wickets. The relentlessness of his attack can be measured by the fact that the great Victor Trumper batted 1 hour and 20 minutes for 29. Douglas finished with 5 for 46 in 17.5 overs, six of which were maidens. It was to be his best bowling in Test cricket.

At tea Australia had lost nine wickets, but the playing conditions decreed that the tea interval must be taken and so the moment of glory was delayed. Shortly after tea, Hordern edged Douglas to Foster at slip and England had won the Ashes. It was for Douglas, and for his team, a very great moment.

There were toasts and speeches after the match. Mr D. McKinnon, President of the Victorian Cricket Association, proposed the health of the England team and congratulated them on their fine performances. It was Pelham Warner who responded, saying that he was disappointed not to have played, but that he congratulated John Douglas on the admirable way in which he had led the side. Douglas' speech was typical of the man. 'A quarter of an hour ago I was the happiest man on earth; now that I have to make a speech I am not.' He gave all the credit to others, to Warner who had guided him off-field, to Foster and the senior players who had helped him on the field.

His handling of his bowlers and his astute field-placings had won applause since the first Test, and he had led the side with good judgment and temper. This most laudatory verdict was from those who considered that the bowling of Foster, Barnes and Douglas in this series was the finest that has ever been seen on good, true wickets. No-one has disagreed with that assessment since.

What remained of the tour was celebratory. There was a

fine victory over New South Wales, and the final Test was won by 70 runs. Barnes finished the series with what was then a record 34 wickets at 22.88 runs each, Foster had 32 at 21.62 and Douglas 15 at 23.66. It had been mighty bowling.

At a special MCC dinner at the Hotel Wentworth, Sydney, during the final Test, the menu was named in honour of the team. The second course was 'Turtle Soup au Douglas (slow but sure)'.

As a captain and as a player, his reputation had increased greatly and it was generally agreed that on Australian wickets he had proved a better bowler than he was in England, but it was also felt that he would now go on improving and become a very great all-rounder.

His men had nothing but praise for him. In spite of that initial upset, Barnes thought him a great man, and Barnes did not give praise lightly. Hobbs was always an admirer and 'Tiger' Smith, in his ninety-third year, remembered with such affection the man who had given him his first chance in Test cricket 68 years before:

> We were all friends together in the party. Never a jealous word passed between any of us and Johnny Douglas deserves all the credit for being such a fine leader. He'd never play the heavy-handed one; he'd let you know well in advance whether you were playing in the next match. If you weren't, he'd say, 'I want you with us for the match after. I don't care where you go or what you do but I want you back, fit and ready for cricket.' He treated us like men and we responded to that. I got on tremendously with Johnny – he took me shooting and fishing for a week in Tasmania halfway through the tour. Imagine it, Tiger Smith from the backstreets of Birmingham hob-nobbing with an amateur educated at Felsted College! But there was no 'side' to Johnny; he was as straight as they come.

There was much celebrating and no doubt John Douglas sipped a few bottles of vintage port. All the praise he directed to Warner whose team, he said, it was. But John Douglas returned to England a hero. He had won both the Ashes and a nickname, 'Johnny Won't Hit Today'. He, and his father, were immensely proud of the achievement and, in the companionship of his friends, he allowed himself a broad grin and gave himself another nickname – 'Johnny Won His Test'.

6
Lean Years

A captain who returns from Australia victorious by four Tests to one could, with good reason, hope to retain the captaincy for at least another Test, but this was not the case in 1912. The amateurs who had not been able to make the trip to Australia were now available and these were not days of sentiment.

Even at the height of Douglas' success in Australia, Pelham Warner had written: 'On this form in Australia Douglas will be very near the England Eleven this summer if the matches are played on hard, true wickets. He has improved immensely.' The inference from Warner's comment is that, in spite of his great success as captain and player in Australia, there was little thought that Douglas would be considered for the Test side when there was a full complement of players to choose from.

He captained the Rest against England in the first Test trial and his side was beaten by an innings. In the second Test trial he played under Warner's captaincy for the MCC Australian XI against the Rest. Warner and Woolley got centuries and Jessop batted well for the Rest, who were beaten by an innings. Douglas scored 41 and bowled C. B. Fry in the first innings.

The selection committee met and C. B. Fry was appointed captain. After that, they disbanded and Fry became the sole selector for the rest of the summer. This was the season of the triangular tournament between England, Australia and South Africa. It was a wet summer and the tournament, an ambitious forerunner of the World Cup, was not a success. For Douglas it was not a good season. He scored more runs than he had ever scored before, 1411, and took 81 wickets, but the cost was high and Essex won only one match, dropping to next but last place in the Championship table.

Essex played the Australians twice. In May, the Australians scored 564 for 3 declared at Leyton and won by an innings. Douglas took 2 for 107 and scored 60 and 53. In the second match, at the end of June, Douglas and Perrin put on 160 for the second wicket, and Douglas and Fane added 183 for the third wicket. Essex scored 421 and only a fine century by Gregory saved the Australians from defeat on the last day. Douglas' 129 was one of two centuries that he hit in the season, for he took 109 off the Lancashire bowling at Leyton a month later.

His best performance with the ball was saved for the last match of the season when he was in the Rest of England side which played the Champion County, Yorkshire, at the Oval. The Rest, led by Spooner, who hit a hundred, won by an innings and Douglas took 7 for 29 in the second innings, six of them clean bowled.

Douglas played in only one Test, the last of the triangular tournament, against Australia at the Oval, and then he came into the side at the very last moment when, on the morning of the first day, Ernie Hayes of Surrey was found to be suffering from a cold. *Wisden* wrote with kindness, 'No place had been found for Douglas in any of the previous Test matches, but he is by temperament so much the man for a big occasion, that he might well have been picked for the whole series.'

There is an indication in C. B. Fry's autobiography, *Life Worth Living*, that Douglas would have played against South

Africa in the match at Headingley if his wife had not been taken ill with appendicitis, although none of the commentators at the time seemed aware of this. Fry considered Leeds to be an unlucky ground for England and lists his reasons:

> In 1921 Jack Hobbs developed appendicitis there, and had to be operated on by Lord Moynihan. And there it was that Johnny Briggs went off his head and never played again; Colin Blythe had an epileptic fit; Gilbert Jessop shockingly ricked his back and was out of cricket for some time; and, in harmony, Mrs. J. W. H. T. Douglas had appendicitis which prevented Johnny from playing.

As the England v. South Africa game at Leeds in 1912 was the only match during Johnny's Test career in which he could have played at Headingley but did not, Fry must be referring to this match, and he was the supremo at the time. There is, however, an inconsistency in Fry's statement. Johnny Douglas was a bachelor until 1916 when he married Evelyn Ruby Case, a widow, and it is likely that the illness that Fry refers to was suffered by John Douglas' mother and not his wife.

Whatever Fry's intentions, Douglas did not play at Leeds, and on Monday 19 August 1912, he represented England in a home Test match for the first time. Remarkably, he did not bowl in the entire match in which Woolley took ten wickets.

England batted first, and when Douglas went in with the score at 144 for 5, he was cheered all the way to the wicket. It was an overwhelming welcome for the man who had brought the Ashes back from Australia; the crowd was saying 'thank you'. He was lbw to Whitty for 18 and England made 245. Barnes and Woolley then bowled Australia out for 111. At close on the third day, England were 64 for 4 and the game was in the balance. Fry had defended doggedly on a wicket that was giving the bowlers every assistance, but next morning he lost Hearne at 91, and still Australia had a chance. Douglas and Fry batted quite magnificently, though, the Essex man giving his skipper just the support he needed. The quality of their batting can be gauged from the fact that once Fry was out, at 170, the four remaining wickets went down for five runs.

Australia were bowled out for 65 and England had won by 244 runs. It was the first timeless Test in England, but it was all over in four days. It was Douglas' fifth consecutive Test as a member of an England side victorious over Australia. He was to play against them 11 more times and never again was he to be on the winning side, but by then times had changed.

1912 was the year in which C. H. 'Pickles' Douglas played his first game for Essex. He was in the side that met Northamptonshire at Northampton in mid-June. Essex were beaten by an innings in two days and were bowled out for 60 and 81, G. J. Thompson and Mr S. G. Smith bowling unchanged throughout the match. 'Pickles' was run out for 0 in the first innings and caught Smith, bowled Thompson for 1 in the second.

'Pickles'' career in cricket was a brief one. He did not play in 1913, played six games in 1914, and then returned after the war. In the two-day matches of 1919, he began to develop. He was in the Essex side for 14 of their 20 matches. For most of the time he batted no. 7 or 8, and in June 1919, he took the last three Kent wickets to fall at a personal cost of 46 runs, a career-best, half the total number of wickets he was to take in first-class cricket. When the side went up to Manchester in July he batted no. 5 and scored 78, his only fifty in first-class cricket. Against Somerset in the next match, he found himself back at no. 7. When Essex went down to Weston-super-Mare in August as part of their West Country tour he was no. 10 in the order.

He confronted brother John and asked what he thought he was doing. 'I got 78 up at Manchester. I should be higher than no. 10.'

'I decide the order' was the only reply that he got.

In that game, 'Pickles' joined John with the score at 200 and the brothers batted together for two hours and saved the follow-on which had been over 50 runs away when the eighth wicket fell. John scored 66 not out and 'Pickles' hit 45. He felt that he had proved his point.

They travelled to Bournemouth for the next match and 'Pickles' asked what number he would be batting.

'No. 10,' said John.

'Bugger that,' said the younger brother and packed his bags and went home.

In fact, he did play again at Clifton at the end of August when he batted no. 8 and scored 2, but he felt that first-class cricket held no further charms for him and he never played again, preferring to concentrate on his first love, boxing.

Perhaps it was asking too much to have two Douglas' temperaments in the same side.

However poor the season of 1912 had been for John Douglas and for Essex, it was as nothing compared to the disasters of 1913. True, Essex won one more match than they had done in the previous season, but they also lost one more match and they remained second to bottom in the County Championship, only Somerset, who also had two wins, finishing below them. Their only victories were both over Sussex, and both in July. In the first match, at Leyton, Douglas took 5 for 46 and 1 for 25 as Essex won by 131 runs, and in the second match, at Brighton three weeks later, Essex won by six wickets and Douglas took 5 for 55 and 4 for 66. Essex's dependence on Douglas can be realised from the fact that their two victories coincided with the only two occasions during the season when he took five wickets in an innings for them.

His best performance in the season was 5 for 40 for MCC against Yorkshire at Scarborough early in September, but his endeavours throughout the year brought him only 68 wickets. It was very strange, for the wickets were harder than they had been in 1912 and therefore much better suited to his pace.

As a batsman he fared even worse. His aggregate for the season was 543 at an average of 14.67. Characteristically, his one fifty of the season was to come against Yorkshire in mid-August. Essex had followed on 397 runs in arrears and then lost 2 for 19. Perrin and Fane added 161 in 2½ hours, but still Essex faced defeat. Claude Buckenham joined Douglas and for an hour and a half they kept the ninth wicket intact before Douglas was the sixth of Drake's seven victims. He had scored a typically stubborn 88, but Essex were still beaten by an innings. It was small comfort in such a miserable year: all things considered, it was the worst season that he was to have for Essex in his entire career.

In the winter of 1913–14, MCC were sending a team to South Africa where England had lost the previous series in 1909–10 by three Tests to two. Once more there was the problem of captaincy. Warner, at 40, was no longer young enough or fit enough to lead a major overseas tour, and neither Fry nor Foster was available. The rich vein of amateurs of the Golden Age was growing thin as the period entered its twilight days.

Lord Harris and his selection committee were delighted at the re-emergence of Gilbert Jessop as an all-round force and they were equally delighted when the 'Croucher' agreed to represent the Gentlemen against the Players, a match in which Douglas failed to distinguish himself. At the beginning of August, Lord Harris wrote to Jessop saying that he was pleased to learn that the Gloucestershire man felt that he might be able to make the trip to South Africa. He also said that F. L. Fane, who had relinquished the Essex captaincy in 1906 and who had captained England in two Tests in South Africa on the last tour, had already been approached with a view to leading the side, and that Fane had said that he would captain the team to South Africa, but reluctantly. When it was believed that Jessop would go, Fane wrote to him and said how pleased he would be if Jessop would captain the side instead of him. By mid-August Lord Harris had heard that Jessop now felt that he would not be able to make the trip so Fane was approached again.

There were only three other amateurs in the party, M. C. Bird of Surrey, D. C. Robinson, the reserve wicket-keeper, from Gloucestershire, and Hon. Lionel Tennyson, who had just burst upon the scene for Hampshire and who will figure more prominently later in the story of J. W. H. T. Douglas. Before the end of August, Fane, who had never been keen on the idea of returning to Test cricket and making another tour, told the selectors that he would be unable to captain the side. Jessop was not to be prevailed upon. His Test career was over and his first-class career drawing to its close. Tennyson was too young, too inexperienced and was yet to captain his county. There was only one man who had the time and the financial support of his father and his company to make it possible for him to go, so they asked him – J. W. H. T. Douglas.

7

The Twilight of the Gods

The team that set sail for South Africa was certainly the strongest that had been sent to the Dominion up to that time. Apart from Douglas and the three other amateurs, Bird, Robinson and Tennyson, there was Hobbs, Strudwick, Mead, Woolley, Rhodes, Booth of Yorkshire, Relf, Hearne and the great Sidney Barnes.

It was customary in those days to give as large a proportion of places as possible to amateurs but, as we have seen, there were not too many of quality available. Morice Bird's Test career was restricted to this tour of South Africa and the previous one four years earlier. In ten Tests he scored 280 runs and took eight wickets, five of them on his first tour. Robinson was destined never to play Test cricket. Indeed, he did not play in a single match on this tour, falling ill as soon as he reached South Africa and being sent home. Almost certainly it was at Douglas' insistence that 'Tiger' Smith was sent out as replacement; the two men had the greatest respect for each other. Smith arrived shortly before the first Test match and was to play in the second, but solely as a batsman. Strudwick kept wicket throughout the series.

The South African side was a shadow of the team that had

beaten England four years earlier, and the great googly quartet of Faulkner, Schwarz, Vogler and White had disappeared. Their most successful bowler on the matting wickets in this series was to be James Blanckenberg with his medium pace. They were led by Herbie Taylor, whose Test career was to last for the best part of another 20 years and who was to remain the undisputed master batsman on matting wickets.

This was to be a triumphant tour for the Englishmen, but it did not begin well. Western Province made 375 in the opening match at Newlands and MCC had to follow on. They saved the game easily, thanks to Hobbs, Hearne and Douglas, who made 61.

There were victories in minor matches before Cape Province were beaten by an innings at Port Elizabeth. Hobbs hit 170, and Douglas took 4 for 26 in the first innings before Barnes routed them in the second. The run of success continued unabated until the first Test. Douglas, who played in every match of the tour, used himself sparingly, often batting low in the order and bowling only a handful of overs so that every player was given a chance to establish himself. The captain played an innings which suggested that he was preparing himself for sterner battles when, just under a fortnight before the first Test, he batted 4¼ hours against Border at East London and scored 102 not out. His innings, as *Wisden* emphasised, contained 39 singles.

The Englishmen reached the first Test full of confidence, and that confidence was fully justified over the next four days. Taylor won the toss and chose to bat. Barnes and Booth opened the bowling and Taylor's opening partner, Hartigan, one of only four players in the South African side who was not making his Test debut, was caught at the wicket off Barnes for 0 with only 5 runs on the board. Taylor alone played Barnes with any confidence, and this was to remain the pattern for the rest of the series.

Barnes took 5 for 57, and in 3 hours 20 minutes, South Africa were bowled out for 182. Taylor was the last man out, caught at the wicket off Johnny Douglas for 109. Douglas also bowled Nourse, the second-top scorer with 19, and his two wickets cost 19 runs. At the end of the first day, England had lost Rhodes and Relf for 94. Next morning Hobbs was out at 136, having batted less than two hours for his 82. Tennyson was out 37 runs later and this brought in Douglas. He batted for 4¼ hours and hit 119. It was his one and only Test century. It was acquired with characteristic patience and determination and it ended on the third morning when rain restricted play to less than an hour. It was the first time in the history of Test cricket that the opposing captains had each scored a hundred.

On the fourth day, Barnes took 5 for 48 and South Africa were beaten by an innings and 157 runs. They fared no better in the second Test when Barnes took 17 wickets, a Test record which was to stand until Jim Laker's 19 wickets at Old Trafford in 1956.

There was no gap between the second Test and the third at Johannesburg at the beginning of January. England led by 87 on the first innings, but they slipped to 84 for 3 in the second innings which caused Douglas to promote himself to no. 5. He added 93 with Phil Mead and he went on to score 77. South Africa needed 396 to win and when Taylor and Zulch began with a stand of 153 it seemed possible, but then Relf broke the stand and Barnes returned to take five wickets. England were held up again by Ward and Blanckenberg, but Douglas dismissed them both and his side had won by 91 runs. With this victory came victory in the rubber.

The team was to win 12 out of the tour's 22 matches and lost only once, against Natal in Durban shortly before the fourth Test, the only Test which England failed to win. Barnes took 14 wickets in the match, but England were chasing a target of 313 on the last day and were 154 for 5 when bad light and rain brought play to a close. It proved to be S. F. Barnes' last Test match, for he was reported unfit for the fifth Test. He had been ill at the beginning of the tour.

In the four Tests in which he played, Barnes took 49 wickets at 10.93 runs each. Douglas, like many others, felt that Barnes stood head and shoulders above the rest and that he had never seen a more magnificent contest than that between Barnes and Taylor. Barnes played one-third of his Test matches under Douglas' captaincy and took 83 wickets in them. He was not an easy man, but he admired Douglas. He thought he was 'straight'.

Without Barnes, England won the final Test by ten wickets. Douglas, who used the new ball only once in the series, in the second Test, took 4 for 14 and 1 for 34. Once more he had led England in triumph and his own contribution had not been a meagre one. His average of 38.00 placed him fourth in the batting averages for the Tests, and his ten wickets at 23.90 were on a par with Relf and, in number, second only to Barnes. Over the tour as a whole, Douglas was second in batting only to Hobbs and in bowling, he had 30 first-class wickets at 17.70 each. *Wisden*'s curt assessment was that 'Douglas had a capital tour both as batsman and bowler.'

The tour was not without its problems, however. Barnes missed the last Test because it was reported that he was confined to his bed, but years later, in the *News Chronicle* of 17 April 1953, Barnes was quoted as saying that he did not play in the final Test because he was at loggerheads with the management – not, he hastened to add, with John Douglas, but with the manager that had been provided for the tour.

MCC, confident of success, had tried to cut expenses for the tour. They sent only 13 players as opposed to the 16 that they had sent to Australia because the South African Cricket

Association was paying the tour expenses and fees of £200. There was no official scorer with the party, and the baggage-man was provided by the South African Cricket Association. So was the manager, Ivor Difford.

From the beginning of the tour it was apparent that Difford was not the man to manage Douglas or any of his players. At Johannesburg there were rumours that the team was drinking heavily. 'Tiger' Smith denied this emphatically and said that the reputation had been gained because Difford had failed to return to host clubs bottles of beer, wine and spirits which had been left for the players' use but which had not been drunk.

Smith also lists Douglas among those who hardly ever touched a drop, but this is rather hard to believe. Douglas kept himself very fit to the end of his life, but he lived well and he drank well. Douglas senior was a great connoisseur of port and John followed in his father's footsteps. There is a tale of old Douglas entertaining in his house at Wanstead and, in jovial mood after dinner, he ordered the butler to bring another bottle of vintage port. 'Don't forget to give it a good shake,' he bellowed, and then roared with laughter. The butler returned in a few minutes with the bottle which he was shaking furiously. Old Douglas stopped laughing. Johnny Douglas was certainly a hard drinker at times, for he did nothing by halves, but Charles Bray said that in the years he knew him, he never saw him the worse for drink.

Barnes' disagreement with Difford was over expenses. Barnes took his wife and son to South Africa with him and insisted that he was told that there would be a collection towards their expenses if he did anything outstanding. As Barnes took 49 wickets in four Tests and 125 wickets at less than ten runs each in all matches, he was entitled to think that he had done something outstanding, but no collection was arranged, which was why he did not play in the final Test.

72

Smith supports Barnes' view of Difford on expenses. In the autobiography that he dictated to Pat Murphy, he said:

> Ivor Difford tried to deduct money from some of the players – he tried to take £50 off me because I hadn't played on the full tour, Bert Relf was £10 short, Phil Mead a fiver and Jack Hearne was short because he'd been in hospital at Durban and the manager thought Jack should pay for that!
>
> There was a hell of a rumpus. Johnny Douglas argued with Difford, made sure I got my £200 and all the other lads got their full whack as well.

There was another cause for debate which was spread by rumours in the press concerning the behaviour of the team. Douglas refuted criticisms in his article for MacLaren's *World of Cricket*, 18 April 1914:

> Lots of things have been said about the team in the papers. I have never been fond of writing to papers, and so I have let them go their own sweet way, not troubling to contradict their stories.
>
> Social functions caused most of the trouble – the newspaper trouble, that is. These social functions are all very well in their way; but they don't help one to do oneself justice on a strenuous tour – such as this was – with so much travelling to be got through. One meets a lot of people, naturally, and they try to do one well, but too much can be had, even of a good thing.
>
> The men were a happy family. I had no occasion to speak to anyone about his behaviour either on or off the field. Bird and Tennyson backed me up loyally, and enjoyed the trip immensely, as indeed all of us did.

The most significant incident to which Douglas alludes was the alleged snubbing of the mayor at Bloemfontein. The memories of Hobbs and Smith are consistent in asserting that there was an unfortunate misunderstanding, that they had expected some sort of official welcome when they arrived but had found none. They learned later that the mayor had been waiting for them at one end of the railway platform and they had left by a different exit. Douglas was severely criticised in the South African press, but he had not been with the party when they arrived, and as soon as he came to Bloemfontein he went straight to the mayor and attempted to heal the wounds caused by the misunder-standings. The Dutch-language press, however, seemed intent on keeping the incident alive.

It was typical of Douglas that whenever there were diffi-culties and his men had problems, he would stand by them and help them in every way. He was not the easiest nor the most tactful of men – he and Barnes had that in common, which is perhaps why they got on well – but there was none more loyal, nor more anxious to preserve integrity.

Hobbs' admiration for him grew year by year:

> J. W. H. T. Douglas was one of the best bowlers with a new ball that I have ever batted against. He could swing in and out. It was difficult to distinguish his in-swinger from the away-swinger. He was one of the greatest triers and whole-hearted players I have ever met – all in and all out, all the time. Every match was a battle to him. Moreover, he was a marvellous companion on tour.

Smith's memory of the tour, in which he played a small part, was that the team spirit was excellent, but that it could not have been anything else under a skipper like Johnny Douglas.

Woolley's memories of that South African tour are very brief, but as the 'ghost' of his autobiography, *The King of Games*, talks of Lord Tennyson as being captain of the party, it is hardly surprising.

On his return to England in April, Douglas talked of the googly as being a thing of the past as everyone was now on the look-out for it. This was wishful thinking. He also stated that no party should go abroad with less than 15 players and that of these, five should be amateurs. He had now played in 11 Test matches, and in ten of them he had been captain. He had been on the winning side nine times and had lost only one game, the first. It was a mighty record. He had scored 410 runs for England and taken 25 wickets, and in the years to come, this record was not to diminish.

But Johnny Douglas was never again to play on a winning side in a Test match, although the chasm that was to separate the tarnished future from the golden present had not yet opened.

Douglas returned in triumph. As the English season of 1914 wore on, his reputation was enhanced. Essex rose to eighth in the Championship table, winning nine matches. For the first time in his career, John Douglas performed the double, 1288 runs at an average of 35.77 and 138 wickets at a cost of 19.10 runs each. For Essex alone, he scored 1151 runs and took 118 wickets and so became the first Essex player to perform the double for the county. He topped the batting averages and was morally top of the bowling averages, only Buckenham's 26 wickets at a fractionally lower cost beating him.

He was still short of his thirty-second birthday and was exuding a confidence born of success. *Wisden*, not given to excesses, was in ecstasy about him. His all-round form 'has perhaps never been approached by an Essex cricketer.' He 'deserved the warmest congratulations on the fact of the side faring so much better than in any year since that in which he took over the captaincy.' In batting he developed considerable versatility.

No-one ever doubted his capacity for hard hitting, but actual freedom came as a surprise more than once to people who could regard him in no other light than as a dogged

defender, possessed of impeturbable patience. More than
once Douglas scored quite fast, but objection to take risks
had become too deep-rooted for him to make a prolonged
effort to punish bowling severely.

Not only was there a new approach to batting, but there was
an enterprise and cavalier approach to captaincy that
surprised many. At Leyton, he won the toss against
Middlesex and asked them to bat. They scored 464 for 1
declared and Essex lost by an innings. He had gambled on
the sun shining on a damp wicket, but the sun did not shine
and the wicket became slow and easy, and the newspapers
chastised him. Undeterred, he put Sussex in to bat on a
drying pitch at Southend. They were bowled out for 102,
but Essex struggled in reply until Douglas batted with 'great
care' for three hours to score 41. Then he took the ball and
bowled unchanged with Tremlin. Sussex were bowled out
for 47 and Douglas had used the wind to great effect for his
away-swinger. He took 6 for 18 in 12 overs.

Surrey, the eventual champions, suffered only one defeat
at the Oval and that was when Essex beat them by 323 runs.
Again the match was a triumph for Douglas. He hit 74 not
out in the first innings and bowled unchanged throughout
the match, taking 6 for 60 and 5 for 38. He clean bowled Jack
Hobbs in both innings.

It was the centenary of the Lord's ground in St John's
Wood, and there was a match between the MCC South
African team and the Rest of England. Douglas' side was
beaten by an innings, but this did not detract from the
splendour of the celebration dinner in the evening at which
he was one of the honoured guests. W. G. Grace received a
marvellous ovation when he rose to speak, and when F. S.
Jackson proposed the toast to the two teams who had taken
part in the centenary match it was C. B. Fry who replied;
Douglas was not much of a hand at speech-making.

The highlight of this memorable season, however, was the Gentlemen v. Players match at Lord's on 13, 14 and 15 July. The Gentlemen won a splendid victory by 134 runs, their first win at Lord's since 'Douglas' match' in 1911, and only their second in eight years. Pelham Warner felt that, in the whole history of the matches, it was doubtful whether the two sides had ever put stronger XIs into the field. Perrin declined an invitation to play for the Gentlemen and Spooner had to withdraw, but Fry led a team which included Warner, Foster, Jessop, Fender and Douglas. Hobbs captained a Players' side which included Hearne, Mead, Gunn, Woolley, Barnes and Strudwick.

Rain on the Sunday had affected the pitch and although the weather was fine on the Monday, the first day, Barnes and Hitch were able to exploit the wicket so that Fry, Hornby, Day and Warner were out for 37. Douglas joined S. G. Smith and he was at the wicket for 20 minutes before he scored. He was patience itself, but he was still active enough to help Smith in an invaluable stand of 66 runs in an hour and a quarter. Smith was brilliantly stumped and Douglas went at 130, but by now the wicket had eased and the Essex captain's patient 22 had made it possible for the later batsmen to gather some cheap runs. He followed this with a splendid opening spell which accounted for Hobbs and Tarrant before the close of play. There was no relaxation on the Tuesday which, according to Warner, produced cricket that was 'the keenest imaginable'.

Douglas bowled, in all, for 3¾ hours of the Players' innings, which lasted for 4½ hours. He kept an immaculate length, gained that mysterious speed off the pitch and moved the ball both ways. Woolley fell to Foster, but the other nine wickets were taken by Douglas: 38.2 overs, 8 maidens, 9 wickets for 105 runs. For most of the time his attack was on the off stump and he maintained a brisk pace throughout. It was an epic piece of bowling. In the matches between the two sides, which lasted for more than 100 years, only two other bowlers, D. Buchanan in 1868 and Captain J. W. A. Stephenson (also of Essex) in 1936, took nine wickets in an innings for the Gentlemen.

The Gentlemen had snatched a lead of nine runs on the first innings, and by the close of the second day they were 148 for 2. In the night there was rain and on the last morning the ball began to jump and turn. Smith, Foster and Fender all showed resilience and the Gentlemen reached 275, so leaving the Players a target of 285 to win.

Foster and Douglas launched a ferocious attack. Douglas made the ball rear menacingly off a length, and he had Hobbs caught behind for 3 and Tarrant caught behind for 0. Foster bowled Hearne for 4, while Douglas bowled Mead for 9 and had Gunn taken at slip by Fender. Woolley fell to Foster and the Players were 28 for 6. Fry kept Douglas and Foster bowling too long, thought Warner, 'in a very laudable and generous desire to let them bowl unchanged', but having bowled for two hours and taken eight wickets between them, they were replaced and Smith finished the job. 'It was as much Douglas' match as it had been in 1911, and his was some of the finest bowling seen in the history of these games.'

Douglas' performance in this match had great influence in having him named as one of *Wisden*'s Five Cricketers of the Year in the 1915 annual, where Fender, S. G. Smith, the Northants captain who had played a big part in the Gentlemen's victory, Hardinge and D. J. Knight joined him. 'The position Mr Douglas now holds in the cricket world,' wrote *Wisden*, 'has been won by sheer hard work and perseverance.'

But even as the Gentlemen were gaining their historic victory, the clouds of war were gathering. Fry, Jessop and Barnes were never again to play in these matches, and the Gentlemen were not to be victorious at Lord's again for another 20 years: their golden age had come to an end.

A fortnight after Douglas' triumph at Lord's, Austria declared war on Serbia. Five days later, Germany demanded that Belgium allow her to march through her country to attack France. Crowds gathered in Whitehall and there were displays of patriotism. None could foresee the trauma that the next four years would bring.

In the first days of war, cricket continued in an air of unreality – business as usual, it would all be over by Christmas. Douglas and Freeman put on 261 for the seventh wicket against Lancashire at Leyton, and in the next game, at Worcester, Russell and Carpenter had a stand of 237. Essex were beaten at Northampton and then Douglas went down with influenza. He returned for the last game, at Weston-super-Mare, but there was no joy now. The Battle of the Marne was only five days away.

It was, indeed, a twilight of the gods, and the Golden Age ended in fire and violence and pain. It is separated from us now by a chasm of suffering and when we peer into its golden mist, we see a time of perpetual sunshine in which the giants of cricket strode the earth, and all was leisure. It was not like that, of course, and what we view is a romantic, distorted picture, but much that has happened since has made it eminently desirable that that distorted image was a reality.

8
War Years

When war broke out, Douglas was at the height of his powers. He was a month short of his thirty-second birthday and his record as cricket captain of England marked him as one of his country's most successful leaders in the history of the game. His own play had been developed to the extent where he had accomplished the double of 1000 runs and 100 wickets in a season for the first time. He had attained the highest honours in two other sports. Financially, he was secure: socially, he was prominent. He was conscious of the dignity of his position, the sense of authority, but he was conscious, too, as were all those of his standing in the days of the Empire, of the responsibilities which that position brought with it. When war was declared, as his old school magazine, *The Moultonian*, expressed it, 'such a sportsman was sure to take the field.'

He enlisted immediately and was commissioned as a second lieutenant in the Bedfordshire Regiment. In March 1915 he was made full lieutenant. It was obvious that a man with such proven qualities of leadership would receive rapid promotion. In November 1915, he became a captain, and in the following year, he rose to non-substantive major and then lieutenant-colonel. In 1917, he was gazetted to the substantive rank of major although, in the years after the war, the title 'Colonel' had the right ring about it for Douglas and it became more like a nickname.

In 1918, his battalion was disbanded and he came home to England for two months. He returned to France and was posted to 3rd Army Headquarters Staff as superintendent of physical training and bayonet training. This was obviously a position well suited to him as, from the early days of the war, he had interested himself in the organisation of army sports and physical fitness programmes. Douglas had the body that one would expect of a champion boxer and he maintained it in peak condition to the very end. He was always training, summer and winter, and subjected his body to the strictest discipline. His fitness became legendary and he was universally known as the fittest cricketer of his day. He expected as much of others, and one can imagine that the men under his command underwent a rigorous training in physical fitness.

'Pickles' followed him into the Bedfordshire Regiment and became a captain. He returned to Moulton Grammar School on occasions to give lectures to the boarders on military matters, and the lectures were remembered as being full of fun and anecdotes.

The records of sporting doings from the first world war are fragmentary, but we know that Douglas participated fully in army football, cricket and boxing. There were some 'international' encounters still. There is an interesting account in *The Larwood Story*, a book which the great England bowler wrote with the assistance of Kevin Perkins in 1964:

In March 1916, when the war was at its height, a cluster of troops on leave renewed memories of more peaceful days when they gathered at the Gezireth Sports Club, Cairo, to watch a cricket match. The game was between a team of English troops and A.I.F. members. Some of the Australians were from the small headquarters staff left in Egypt after the Gallipoli evacuation, the rest were light-horsemen training

81

for the campaign which eventually was to beat the Turks in Palestine.

The odds were on the Tommies. Several had played for English counties and their captain, Colonel J. W. H. T. Douglas, was the celebrated Johnny Douglas who had led England to victory against Australia and South Africa.

Expecting an easy win, the Englishmen weren't prepared for the shock they got from a big and powerfully built light-horseman who was brought in from the Suez Canal and dressed for the match simply by discarding hat, shirt and leggings.

Apologizing for being a bit out of practice, the Australian skittled the Tommies with short-pitched bumpers, yorkers that knocked bats out of some hands, full tosses which broke a couple of stumps and occasional good-length balls. Most were out before scoring. He then pasted the bowling all over the field before retiring to catch a train back to Suez.

The Australian tearaway bowler was 'Tibby' Cotter, who was to be killed by a sniper's bullet in the campaign against the Turks a year later, and although the story has a hint of the apocryphal, it would have been typical of Douglas that he would be engaged in organising such a match.

One thing is certain and that is that John Douglas was in England for Christmas 1916, for on Christmas Day he married Evelyn Ruby Case whose first husband, an army officer, had died in March 1911. The couple had met in Northampton, which was one of the focal points for amateur boxing in the days before the first world war. Douglas, as a leading personality in the sport, was a frequent guest of Evelyn Case's brothers, who were sporting enthusiasts, and it was through them that the link between Evelyn and John was forged.

She brought with her to their marriage a twelve-year-old son, Gerald, who was destined for a career other than cricket or boxing. 'I have sparred a few rounds with the old man,' he recalls, 'but I don't remember ever laying a glove on him although he certainly hurt me.' In his flat near Ascot, Gerald Case still has in his possession a silver cigarette box which was presented to the couple on the occasion of their marriage by the officers of the Bedfordshire Regiment.

Evelyn Case was a positive and forthright woman with a sense of position. She attended many functions with her husband, but they tended to lead independent lives, which suited both their natures.

In 1917, Douglas played at Lord's. This was in the first of two charity matches which had been arranged at the height of summer. It was a match between an England Army XI and an Australian Imperial Forces XI. The England Army XI was led by Captain P. F. Warner, who had Lieutenant-Colonel J. W. H. T. Douglas as his second-in-command again. The Australians were captained by C. G. Macartney, the 'Governor General'. The home side was victorious in a game which saw some good cricket, but which was played in rather a sedate manner. Douglas batted no. 5 and was bowled by C. T. Docker for 20. Opening the bowling with Colin Blythe, he had Macartney lbw for 0.

There was a second charity game a month later, but neither Douglas, because of military duties, nor Makepeace could play in the second match. The Army XI was a strong team and included Harry Lee, Hendren, Lieutenant Percy Fender, Captain W. B. Franklin, Ernest Tyldesley and Colin Blythe. Blythe was killed in action in France three months after the second charity match.

Encouraged by the success of these matches, from which the St Dunstan's Hostel for the Blind benefitted, Warner and the MCC arranged further matches for 1918. Douglas was unable to play in the first England v. Dominions match because of military duties once more, but he played in the game at the Oval on August Bank Holiday Monday. For the first time since 1914 a shilling entrance fee was charged and a large crowd gathered although the weather was far from kind. Herbie Taylor, A. G. Moyes, Pellew and Macartney were in the Dominions side which made 194 for 9 declared, Douglas failing to get a wicket in his nine overs. England began disastrously and when Fender joined Douglas at twenty to seven the score was 75 for 6. 44 minutes later Fender was bowled by Moyes and the score was 162. Of the 87 runs that had been put on, Fender had scored 70. Johnny Douglas was undefeated at 7.30 with 22 runs to his credit. Knox had also been bowled by Moyes, and England finished at 166 for 8. Whatever else was changing in the world, the durability of John Douglas was constant.

He played several matches for the Aldershot Command Cricket Club with considerable success, and it was ironic that he now found himself back at the place where, nearly two decades earlier, he had become a schoolboy boxing champion.

Ironies continued. On 31 August 1918, there was great excitement at Lord's as, for the benefit of Chevrons Club, Captain P. F. Warner's XI was to meet Colonel F. S. Jackson's XI. Sir Stanley Jackson was then 48 years old and had not been seen in first-class cricket for 11 years. 8000 people came to see his return, but he was unwell and felt that he could not make the return to the cricket field that he had promised. Another captain was needed and there was only one obvious choice – J. W. H. T. Douglas. Jack Hobbs played a marvellous innings of 86, and Warner's team made 244. Douglas had 0 for 35 in 11 overs. Jackson's, now Douglas', team were bowled out for 83, and when they batted again they made 129 for 9. Douglas was caught Hardinge, bowled Fender for 16 in the first innings, and in the second innings, he was bowled by a schoolboy named Greville Stevens for 1. In Douglas' own side, there was a young man from Ireland named C. S. Marriott who bowled eight interesting overs. And in 1914 Douglas had thought that the googly was dead!

84

As the last summer of the first world war drew to its close, Grace was dead and Trumper was dead, and William Booth, who had been with Douglas in South Africa, had fallen on the Somme in 1916. G. B. Davies, who had scored two hundreds for Essex in the last weeks before the outbreak of war, was gone, and so was Hutchings of Kent. Two of that great South African googly quartet, Schwarz and White, were dead, and so were thousands more. The world was a much sadder place when the armistice was signed on 11 November 1918, but it proved to be no wiser in spite of the sacrifice of a generation of young men.

Those who had survived were to carry scars, mental and physical, for the rest of their lives, but the immediate hope was to shape a world fit for heroes to live in. In an attempt to re-assert an old order, the psychological changes that had been wrought upon mankind were not fully comprehended. There was a realisation that change of some sort was necessary, but what? In cricket, they thought that the answer was matches which lasted two days instead of three.

9
The Turn of the Screw

There was buoyancy in the air in that summer of 1919, but it was mingled with a weariness. The experiment of playing two-day county matches was not a success and it was abandoned after one season.

There was an older look about the Essex side. Mead's career had ended, and the careers of Carpenter, Fane and McGahey were drawing to their close. Essex had a poor year. They won two matches and finished fourteenth out of fifteen in the championship, Worcestershire having decided not to enter the competition.

In all matches, Douglas again did the double. The war, it seemed, had left him quite unaltered. 'He was the same excellent and indefatigable cricketer as ever,' *Wisden* reported, 'standing the long hours of play much better than many younger men.' In bowling, he had Louden to help him, but there was little else. Only Rhodes, Hitch, Rushby and Kennedy sent down more overs in the season. Only Rhodes and Hitch took more wickets than his 136. Inevitably, he rose to the great occasions. His best bowling of the season was his 8 for 49 for the Gentlemen against the Players at Lord's. 'For the third time in his career,' said *Wisden*, 'Douglas did great things at Lord's for the Gentlemen. Swerving a little and keeping an irreproachable length, he was at his very best.'

It was in 1919 that the Australian Imperial Forces side gave England warning of what was to come. Douglas played against them in their first match, taking seven wickets for Mr Lionel Robinson's XI at Attleborough. He played against them in their second match, too, but with much less success as Essex were beaten by an innings at Leyton. In June, MCC were beaten by ten wickets at Lord's, but Douglas did not bowl in the match. The most important game of the tour was at Lord's a fortnight later when the Australians suffered their first defeat of the tour, at the hands of the Gentlemen of England. Douglas hit 56 and took eight wickets in the match. He was even more successful when the AIF came to Southend for the second match with Essex, taking 7 for 50 and 4 for 168, but the visitors won by 309 runs.

The AIF won 12 and lost four of their 28 matches. Collins and J. M. Taylor each scored over 1000 runs, and Collins and J. M. Gregory both took more than 100 wickets; these were players new to England and to Douglas, but they were to stamp their names indelibly on the minds of all within the next few years.

First-class cricket reverted to three-day matches in 1920, and Essex had a much better season, rising to ninth in the table. Their captain did the double again and, in taking 147 wickets in all matches, had what was to be his best season with the ball, but there were rumbles of criticism. He bowled twice as many overs as any other Essex bowler; Eastman played his first matches this season, and Nichols' debut was still three years away. Douglas seemed to take more and more upon himself, but he saw neither the talent nor the willingness among some of the younger men to share the responsibilities. Supremely fit, totally committed, Douglas could not understand why others did not have these qualities. His belief in himself and in the traditional values in which he was grounded was to remain unshaken until his death, and those who knew him were the richer for it.

Following his wonderful bowling in the Gentlemen v. Players match of 1919, which was drawn in spite of Hobbs' fine hundred and a blistering attack by Douglas and Falcon at the beginning of the Gentlemen's second innings, Douglas wrote to Gilbert Jessop, who had been unwell. The letter, now in David Frith's magnificent collection of cricketana, gives some flavour of the man's endeavour:

'John H. Douglas & Co.   45 Mildmay Chambers,
etc etc   69 Bishopsgate,
            London E.C. 2

            23 July, 1919

My dear Jessopus,
 Ever so many thanks for your kind letter of congrats. I had a little luck first bowl but not the second. Atfield [the umpire] was ———— awful. Still, things even themselves up in the long run. I am awfully sorry to hear you are so queer and I do so hope ere long you will be your old self. Essex are coming down to Weston-s-M on the 11/12th try and run over to see us. All the best old bird
    Yours ever
    Johnny Douglas'

He vibrated with enthusiasm, and *Wisden* appreciated this in its assessment of the 1920 season and the lack of support that Douglas had been given.

The veteran element in the side militated sadly against brilliant work in the field, and the bowling depended to an alarming extent on Douglas who, except on rare occasions from Louden, received no support that was even ever approximately up to first-rate county form. Douglas himself worked untiringly . . . . Only a man of exceptional strength and stamina could have got through such an amount of work. He was inclined to depend too much on his own bowling, but as a matter of fact he had little choice in the matter. He bowled so much better than the other men in his team that he could not afford to keep himself off for long together.

We need look at only one match to indicate the way in which Douglas' enthusiasm and endeavour could carry his team when all seemed lost. This was the year, 'Plum' Warner's last season, in which Middlesex took the Championship by winning their last nine county matches. The last defeat that they were to suffer was at Leyton at the end of July. Leyton always had the reputation of being a paradise for batsmen (and this is where Douglas took his wickets), but on this occasion, the pitch gave a little help to the bowlers. It certainly seemed to aid the Middlesex bowlers. Douglas opened with Russell and was soon caught behind to start a procession back to the pavilion. McIver (43) and McGahey (44) were the only batsmen to reach double figures. They added 70 for the sixth wicket, but Essex were all out for 133 which included 15 byes and 10 leg-byes, an indication of the spark in the wicket on that opening morning.

The Middlesex first innings had an air of unreality about it, for on the second afternoon, both Douglas and Warner had to attend a selection meeting at Lord's. Warner joined Harry Lee after the dismissal of Haig and Hearne, but he had to retire when he had made 22 so that he could journey to the meeting, and Douglas left the field for the same reason after bowling four overs. Hendren and Mann were out as soon as Warner had left the ground, but Lee battled on and Middlesex took a first-innings lead of 79. This was a formidable lead on such a doubtful wicket and, although they batted with more determination in their second innings, Essex again struggled. It was Hearne who troubled them this time with his spin, taking 8 for 49. Perrin, 50, and Douglas, 36, were the top scorers as Essex were dismissed for 196.

Middlesex needed 118 to win. The wicket was not good,

but it was certainly not as bad as it had been on the opening morning, and the Middlesex task was not a difficult one. It was such a challenge as this that Douglas relished. He only admitted defeat when the last run had been scored or the last wicket had fallen. As he rubbed the ball on his forearm on his way back to the end of his run, his dynamic personality bristled with uncompromising aggression. He bounded in, long and rhythmical, his black hair, meticulous and shiny, gleaming like some darker Excalibur. He attacked with every ball, and those of his side who could not respond to his animating fire were left floundering in his wake. There was menace in the air. The Douglas break-back was as famous as it was vicious. Suspect it you might, but to deal with it was another matter. Lee, Haig and Stevens were bowled; Hearne, Hendren and Mann were palpably lbw. 33 for 6.

Warner held on grimly. He had scored 1 when he put a ball from Douglas straight into the hands of forward short leg, whom history has allowed to remain anonymous. He put down the simplest of chances. Douglas swore vehemently and gestured angrily. One cannot be wedded so passionately to the fate of every ball and accept human fallibility or negligence lightly. He took a brief rest. Russell had Skeet lbw, and Louden bowled Gunasekara. 67 for 8. Wicket-keeper Murrell joined Warner in a brave stand. Warner took Douglas' bowling upon himself, leaving Murrell to score as freely as he could the other end. They added 35 before Murrell was lbw to Russell. Warner had only Durston left to help him to score 16 runs.

The duel between Warner and Douglas was an epic one, the energetic, thinking and positive bowler against his ageing, frailer mentor who was a batsman of intelligence and dignified determination. In essence, it was a contest left over from the Golden Age, the last of the wine from a vintage summer. As the sun now blazed down Warner looked a slighter figure. Douglas remained unquenchable, inexhaustible. Durston defended resolutely and Warner made some runs.

With five runs needed for victory and Warner on 46, the veteran faced Douglas who beat him with a fast yorker which scattered the stumps. 'Douglas bowled very finely indeed to win the game for his side,' said *Wisden*. Warner thought it some of the finest bowling that he ever played against. The whole Essex side erupted, caught up by their captain's enthusiasm as he danced with joy. He had taken 7 for 47, the first seven batsmen on the scorecard. Douglas and Warner left the field with their arms round each other's shoulders. They were to be opposed to each other once more, in the match between the Champion County and the Rest of England at the end of the season, but it was that day at Leyton that marked the end of an era.

If it was the end of contests with Warner, it marked the beginning of great contests with Herbert Sutcliffe. It was in 1920 that Sutcliffe carried his bat through the innings for the first time; it was against Essex at Southend. Sutcliffe's memory of that innings was dominated by Johnny Douglas' antics at the batsman's luck.

I was in a knot most of the time, beaten so completely that often I played at the swinging ball to miss it by inches. In the first three-quarters of an hour of the 'hard labour' to which I was put that day I began to wonder if I should ever middle a ball. Time and again I played at the ball only to miss it. Each time J.W.H.T. flung his arms high to protest silently against the foulness of his luck, and finally, at the end of an over about which I had known very little, he came up to me and exploded: 'Why the hell don't you get a bite?'

I got a bite in the next over all right, but it was simply a matter of adding insult to injury, for the ball shot from the edge of my bat to second slip who very kindly put it on to the ground. 'Johnny's' face was a picture. . . .

I believe that if at Southend that glorious day Douglas had

possessed a revolver he would have shot the fieldsmen first
and then turned his attention to me. However, my wretched
innings continued on the lines on which it had started, and
by the time I had 100 runs against my name in the scorer's
book I had given at least two other chances.

In the end, I carried out my lucky bat for 125, and that
night when I had dined with J.W.H.T. and a few friends I
heard all about it. My innings was the sole topic of con-
versation, and the comments and observations on it and my
luck were such that I began to wish I had got out the first ball
sent to me.

It was always a great joy to play against Mr Douglas,
whose love for the game was as great as could be. He was a
fighter second to none, he was a great all-round cricketer,
and he was as charming a gentleman as ever donned flannels.

Sutcliffe's hundred, lucky or otherwise, would have been
ample excuse for John Douglas to have arranged a
celebratory dinner and a bottle or two of vintage port.
Charles Bray remembered that after his first innings in first-
class cricket in which he scored 27, John Douglas considered
it a good enough debut to warrant a bottle of vintage port
with dinner that evening.

It was during the first match of Southend Week, the
match against Derbyshire, that Douglas learned that he was
to captain the MCC side to Australia in the winter of
1920–21, so that the dinner to which Sutcliffe alludes could
have been something of a double celebration, coming as it
did only two days after Lord Harris had travelled to
Southend to inform Douglas that he was to lead the side.

The meeting at Lord's for which Warner and Douglas had
left the match at Leyton on 26 July was the final selection
meeting before the tour party was announced. Warner was
not a member of the selection committee, but he was asked
to go in an advisory capacity, and Douglas attended as a
senior amateur who had been the last man to captain England.

In fact, the captaincy of the England side to tour Australia in 1920–21 was first offered to Reggie Spooner. Spooner played six games for Lancashire in 1920 with a highest score of 63, and the first quarter of this century is littered with his declining of invitations to play in representative cricket matches. He was two years older than Douglas and he had played in one Test match fewer, but he was always a graceful, legendary figure even before Sir Neville Cardus immortalised him.

D. J. Knight and G. E. C. Wood had said that they were unable to tour and the party that was announced on 26 July was R. H. Spooner, J. W. H. T. Douglas, P. G. H. Fender, Rhodes, Hobbs, Woolley, Hendren, Hearne, Russell, Strudwick, Barnes, Howell, Waddington, Makepeace and Dolphin. Barnes rejected the terms that he was offered and Parkin was brought in to replace him. This was a grievous blow, for it is apparent on looking at the original selection that the bowling was by far the weakest department of the side with much resting on Douglas and Barnes. One must recall that nine years earlier Rhodes had not taken a first-class wicket in Australia although much more was expected of him as a bowler now.

Douglas' record as captain spoke for itself and, after 60 years, it is difficult to understand why he was not appointed from the start unless, in their desire to have Spooner make the trip, MCC were obliged to give the captaincy to the more senior player.

It was on 16 August that Spooner's withdrawal from the side became public knowledge and it was then that Lord Harris travelled to Southend, and Douglas' appointment was announced on 18 August. There was a surprising lack of enthusiasm about Douglas taking on the leadership, but there was a sceptical view about the whole tour, most judges feeling, rightly, that neither England nor her cricketers had recovered sufficiently from the Great War to undertake such a venture. A similar feeling was to prevail, also rightly, 25 years later.

The doubt that persisted with regard to Douglas was allied to his conservatism, his lack of flair, but this criticism was based upon his performances with Essex where his resources were very limited. In any case, there was no other obvious candidate for the job. Fender was too inexperienced. His Test career, however short, lay ahead of him, as did his success as Surrey's captain. In 1920, Fender stood in relation to the captaincy of England much in the same position as John Barclay and Geoff Cook stood in 1982 when their names were being put forward before either had established himself as a Test player.

The Times, in announcing the appointment, said that the offer had been made to Douglas directly the MCC knew that Spooner would be unable to go, that another player would be added to the party and that the new player would, if possible, be an amateur. E. R. Wilson was in fact added to the list the next day, and in September, it was decided to take one more player and Hitch was chosen, V. W. C. Jupp being unable to make the trip.

The Times outlined Douglas' career in its brief column which was headed 'Colonel Douglas Accepts the Captaincy'. It stated that he had first been regarded 'as a good bowler and a very bad batsman', but that it was typical of the man that he refused to recognise the fact. 'By sheer perseverance and grit – he even resorted to net practice in the garden – Colonel Douglas made himself into a first-class cricketer.' His popularity was undoubted, but the final paragraph showed *The Times*' uncertainty:

Colonel Douglas's abilities as a captain – like his ability as a player – are self-made and sound rather than brilliant. Perhaps his chief fault is lack of imagination, and an inability to realise that few men are possessed of his own inexhaustible stamina and keenness. But he is sufficiently shrewd, and very much a man.

No doubt, had Douglas been able to answer this criticism, he would have said that no man should be playing for England unless he was fired by a keenness comparable to his, but he had to remain silent and accept the England captaincy for the third time on tour – again as second choice.

On this occasion he was accompanied by his wife and his parents, and although the send-off was as noisy as it had been a decade earlier, there was caution in the air among the many followers of the game who believed this tour to be premature.

The first results of the tour gave no indication of the disasters that were to follow, though: Makepeace got a hundred at Perth, Russell and Hearne scored hundreds in Adelaide, and Parkin took 8 for 55 in the first South Australian innings. Howell took four wickets in the second innings and MCC had an innings victory. There was another innings win in Melbourne where Hobbs and Hendren made hundreds and Rhodes and Woolley spun Victoria out for 85 in the second innings.

The first hint of impending disaster came at Sydney. Hobbs hit 112, Douglas and Fender took three and four wickets respectively, and MCC led by 83 on the first innings. MCC made 250 in their second knock, so leaving New South Wales a target of 334. In three hours, Macartney and Collins put on 244 for the first wicket, and the State side moved to an easy victory by six wickets. Nine of that New South Wales side were to be in the party to come to England the following year, and had Kelleway been able to accept the invitation, it would have been ten.

Douglas made 0 and 10 in the match and each time he fell to Mailey. Few people were ever at ease with Mailey's buzzing, bouncing leg-breaks and googlies, and Douglas suffered more than most. He would study the Australian spinner through binoculars, but it did him little good. He could never spot the googly and would be contorted in his efforts to play the ball. The two men had the greatest respect for each other. They played the game toughly and there was joy in them. Mailey recalled an incident with Douglas on the 1920–21 tour:

> One day in Sydney, Johnny Douglas, the England captain, asked me to show him my hand. He held it for a while and then said, 'Arthur, you've been using resin. I'll report you to the umpire.'
>
> I asked him to show me *his* right hand, and looking at the thumb-nail I noticed it was worn to the flesh on the outside.
>
> 'You've been lifting the seam, Johnny,' I said.
>
> My co-rebel grinned and the matter was dropped.
>
> On the following day I read in the paper: 'Douglas and Mailey appear to be good friends again. They were shaking hands out in the middle yesterday.'

The big defeat in Sydney was looked upon as only a temporary setback when MCC beat Queensland by an innings, Douglas scoring 84. He made 0 in the second match in Brisbane, against quite a strong Australian XI, but he took 5 for 45. There were two minor games before the first Test, neither of which presented any problems. MCC scored 702 against New South Wales Colts, so the big encounter was not approached with any great fear.

England's hopes were justified when Australia were bowled out for 267. Russell went quickly, but Hobbs, Hendren and Woolley played well, and at one time England were 140 for 3. Then wickets tumbled. Douglas made 21 before being stumped off Mailey, but England were all out for 190. The Australian second innings lasted nine hours and they made 581; Collins hit 100 and Warwick Armstrong scored 158 out of 246 in under 3½ hours. England made 281, a reasonable score, but they had needed 659 to win.

Douglas made 119 in a minor match which separated the first Test from the second in which he had no such success, scoring 15 and 9, and taking 2 for 83 as England lost by an innings.

Now there were rumours of dissent in the side. Hearne had been taken ill during the second Test and did not play again on the tour. The side was two down in the series and the fact that Douglas had his parents travelling with him meant that he spent less time with the team off the field than was his custom. He had not produced any real form on the tour as yet, and it was obvious that a change in the tactics or approach of the side was necessary. There were suggestions that Fender should come into the side, even a suggestion that Douglas should stand down and that Fender should lead the side. It is doubtful if this was a very serious suggestion. Hobbs who, with Douglas, Rhodes and manager Toone, formed the selection committee, did not mention it in his memoirs although he mentioned the unease expressed at the council of war in 1911.

Douglas' problem as a captain on this tour was his inability to realise initially that things were not as they had been ten years earlier. There was no Barnes to strike fear and uncertainty into Australian hearts. There was no Foster to zip the ball off the pitch in that embryo leg-theory attack of his. Douglas himself was nine years older than when he had last captained England to victory in Australia. He was a man more certain of his own position than he had been then and perhaps this confidence brought liabilities with it. He was less willing to confer, less willing to seek advice, more despotic. E. W. Swanton's assessment of the tour and the leadership in *A History of Cricket* is difficult to counter:

Douglas had many of the qualities most to be admired in a cricketer, but he was by all account a dull captain whose over-reliance on fast and fastish bowling and general paucity

97

of ideas outweighed, in a long, gruelling series, the value of his own enthusiasm and unflagging example. It was not this time, as it had been nine years earlier, a matter of giving the ball to Barnes and F. R. Foster and leaving them to do the job, with regular spells of relief from himself. In 1920–21 Douglas was surrounded, as it happened, by several men of unusual cricket intelligence, and it is not hard to suppose that the frustration they felt was ultimately reflected in their performances.

Swanton's comment has the advantage of historical hindsight, but only in not emphasising the limitations of the material available to Douglas does he do the captain an injustice. Parkin took 16 wickets in the Tests, but they cost him 41.87 runs each. Fender topped the Test averages with 12 wickets at 34.16. No side can win a Test series when wickets are that expensive. The wickets that Douglas, Woolley, Rhodes and Howell took all cost more than 50 runs apiece. Waddington topped the tour bowling averages in all matches; his one Test wicket cost 118 runs.

Fender was brought into the side for the third Test which, for a time, looked as if it might go England's way. Parkin took five wickets and Australia were out for 354. They were aided by some poor catching. Russell hit 135 not out, Johnny Douglas scored 60 and Frank Woolley 79, and England took a lead of 93 on the first innings. Then came another Australian deluge of runs. Centuries came from Kelleway, Armstrong and Pellew in a total of 582 and, in spite of a century from Hobbs, England fell to Mailey and were beaten by 119 runs.

There was some respite now, and with the Ashes lost, there was only honour remaining. Douglas hit a century against Victoria and another against South Australia in the last match of the tour, but by then honour had been lost and England had suffered the worst beating ever suffered by a side in a series since Test matches first began. There was an eight-wickets defeat in the fourth Test when the skipper played innings of 50 and 60, and there was a nine-wickets defeat in the last Test when he scored 32 not out and 68. Characteristically, he had died bravely. Only Hobbs scored more runs than he in the Tests and only Hobbs had a better average.

At home, the news of the defeats in the Test matches was received with shock and horror. It was not until later, as *Wisden* recorded, that it was realised quite what Douglas and his men had been up against:

> As the news came to hand of defeat after defeat, people thought the Englishmen must be playing very badly. Not till the Australians came here in the summer and beat us three times in succession on our own grounds did we fully realise the strength of the combination that had set up such a record.

There was no question of any blame being attached to Douglas, but there was some criticism of Fender and Wilson who sent home reports of the tour to the press, reports which were not always kindly received by their colleagues. Their activities led to a new ruling which proscribed tourists from conducting journalist's activities, and Fender's future career at Test level certainly suffered because of his actions on this tour.

Parkin remembered the tour with the greatest affection:

> I could never wish to travel with a finer gentleman than our skipper . . . . I am sure my opinion of him is shared by every member of the English team on that tour. Mr Douglas was a charming fellow, and words fail me in expressing my appreciation of him.
>
> What a great skipper he was. He had the heart of a lion and he was the best swing bowler I have ever seen. He could swing a ball either way. His pace was fast-medium, and

batsmen did not know which way the ball would swing. Douglas kept himself in the pink of condition, as one would expect a former world champion boxer to do, and he had a gymnasium at his home. His sisters could box as cleverly as a man, and I would not have put on gloves with them for any money!

Parkin, not an easy man for many people, appreciated Douglas' concern for the social life of his team. There were social gatherings when Parkin was called upon to play his card tricks with Douglas as impresario, and there were the occasions when the team were guests at boxing shows where Douglas acted as referee. For most, Johnny Douglas was a remarkable personality, a fine leader of men and a wonderful companion. In Australia in 1920–21, those qualities were not enough to make him a successful captain of the England cricket team.

There were dissenting notes, and it is right that one should note them. W. H. Ferguson, the scorer and baggage-man, did not appreciate Douglas' treatment of him as a personal servant and singled Douglas out for attack in his memoirs, *Mr Cricket*, published in 1957:

> J. W. H. T. Douglas represented the 'old school' of English Test captains, and I am very thankful that cricket has graduated from that school. 'Johnny-Won't-Hit-Today' Douglas had me chasing all over the Australian continent after him, and I am certain he regarded me, not as baggage-master-scorer, but as his personal batman. As if that were not bad enough, he took several members – male and female – of his family on tour with him, and I had to act as nurse-maid to them, too. Cricket bags and golf clubs are the normal problems of a baggage-master, but I felt like drawing the line when I was made responsible for outsize hatboxes, or ladies' underwear!

Some of this, the last phrase for example, is obviously the

literary licence of Ferguson's 'ghost', but his complaints earlier in the book that the England captain expected him to be at his hotel room at eight every morning have a ring of authenticity about them, as do his comments that Douglas expected his pads and boots cleaned every day of the week, even for practice sessions. There was nothing slovenly or unkempt about Johnny Douglas.

It was a traumatic time for English cricket. Defeat had been not unexpected, but the size of the defeat was humiliating. In 1912, Douglas had returned from Australia triumphant, but with Fry ready to reclaim his throne. Now he returned to sympathy. His was the spirit and character that the time of adversity welcomed. 'The better team won,' he said. 'We have had a punch on the nose; but we know how to take it.'

A passage from the *Morning Post* of 24 January 1921 perhaps captures best the sentiment of the time:

> In the playing field of Moulton Grammar School, near Spalding, stands a tree with the letters J.W.H.T.D. cut in the bark. This was the handiwork of the Captain of the English XI when he was a scholar at Moulton and many of the boys regard the tree as the School's most valuable asset. When the news of England's defeat arrived, one little Douglas worshipper betook himself to this sacred tree in his disappointment. Never for a moment did his faith in his hero waver, but as he stood before the letters he poured forth the following lament: 'Poor old Duggie! But it wasn't your fault. It was the toss those beastly Kangaroos kept winning that lost us the Ashes.'

10
The Year of Rejection

'During all the years I have edited *Wisden* there has never been a season so disheartening as that of 1921.' So wrote Sidney Pardon in the 1922 annual. Few would disagree with him. On his journey to England, Warwick Armstrong predicted that his Australian team would beat England as convincingly in England as they had done in Australia. He was not far wrong: Australia won the first three Tests and England used 30 players in five Test matches. The direction in which English cricket was heading was hard to determine.

There were some bizarre decisions. At the end of June, in the Gentlemen v. Players match, Durston of Middlesex bowled superbly. He was called from the field on the last afternoon and told that the selectors had been so impressed with him that he was to join the England side at Leeds for the third Test which began the following morning. He went home, collected his things and caught the train to Leeds. He did not play in the Test, nor did he ever play for England again.

His county relied heavily on Douglas in 1921, and his absences through Test calls and his sister's illness left Essex with a void which they could not fill. They slumped to fifteenth in the Championship, yet for Douglas himself, it was in many ways a vintage year. He was a Deputy Lieutenant of the County of Essex. He scored more runs in a season than he scored at any other time in his career, 1547, and he took 130 wickets. He played the highest innings of his career, 210 not out, against Derbyshire at Leyton. It was a match to remember.

It was played on 25, 26 and 27 May. The first Test began on 28 May. Douglas opened the bowling when Derbyshire took first knock, but he met with no immediate success. Then he dismissed both openers, Hill-Wood and Oliver, and the rout of Derbyshire had begun. He took 9 for 47 as they were bowled out for 114, and he was not to better these figures in the rest of his career.

Essex lost five wickets for 37 runs and seemed to have little hope of doing any better than Derbyshire had done. By the end of the first day, they were 138 for 7 with Douglas and McIver batting. Douglas continued in fine form the next day. Hare, in his first county game, scored 98 at no. 10, and Essex reached 396 for 9 declared. Douglas batted for 5¼ hours and hit 28 fours in the only double-century of his career. Nor was his part in the match over yet. He withheld himself from the attack as Derbyshire struggled to save an innings defeat. When it seemed likely that they might avoid it he brought himself on. With his third ball he had top scorer Cadman lbw and with his fifth ball he had last man Bestwick caught behind to give Essex one of their five wins in the season.

The season had started splendidly for Douglas and England supporters were heartened by such a marvellous all-round performance by the skipper on the eve of the first Test. He had already tasted Australian blood when, in the second match of their tour, at Attleborough, he had taken 6 for 64 and scored 41 not out for Mr L. Robinson's XI. Then he had scored 3 and 47 not out and taken 2 for 48 when Essex lost by an innings to the Australians at Leyton. He was not in the MCC side which lost narrowly at Lord's, but he had already done enough to suggest that he would be a harder proposition for the Australians in his own country than he had been in Australia.

His appointment as captain of England was, for the first time, unopposed. He was first choice and, to most people, the only possible choice. In a column dedicated to the news of his appointment and accompanied by a cartoon captioned 'A Rough Sea but a Calm Pilot', *The Cricketer* outlined his career and was sharp to note his character:

> He is a great man on a great occasion, and when a crisis has to be faced. For coolness he has few superiors, and he is determination and perseverance incarnate. The only thing that seems to upset him is when he has beaten the batsman and just missed the wicket. On such occasions he is apt to throw his arms about. Extraordinarily strong, he is a picture of physical fitness, and however stern and exciting the contest, his hair is always smooth and beautifully brushed. . . . He had a hard row to hoe on his last tour in Australia, but he never lost heart, and his pluck and grit earned him the unstinted admiration of his opponents, and we have heard him described by one of his team as 'a grand fellow'.
>
> He has many assets as a captain, the chief of which is his refusal to give in until the last ball has been bowled; but he cannot be called a great tactician, as he occasionally takes some time to see the obvious. But he has had a large experience of Australian cricket and cricketers in a hard school on this last tour, and he must have profited enormously thereby. So we believe that he will make a good leader for England, and, in any case, he has our very best wishes for his side's and his own personal success. He is the essence of good temper and impeturbability, if rather too set on his own point of view.

There is a tinge of apprehension and of resignation here, and there is certainly no hint of optimism, but none could have been prepared for what was to happen at Trent Bridge on 28 and 30 May.

England began with the disadvantage of being able to call upon neither Hobbs, who was injured and was destined to play no part in the series, nor Hearne, who was not fully recovered from the illness he had suffered in Australia. In a bright, sun-drenched summer, the first morning of the first Test was chilly and grey. Armstrong considered the wicket, which was hard and plumb if freshened by a little drizzle, to be unsuitable for Mailey and omitted him from the XI. Douglas won the toss and England had probably their last moment of happiness for the rest of the summer when Knight and Holmes, two openers new to Test cricket, took nine runs off Gregory's first over, a single to Knight and two fours to Holmes. Then in one over Gregory removed Knight, Ernest Tyldesley and Hendren: England were 18 for 3, and English cricket was back in the dark ages.

Douglas came in ahead of Woolley, no doubt to face the firing before his men – he would have been first up the ladder in the wars of the middle ages. He scored 11 and he and Holmes added 20. Armstrong knew Douglas' weakness against leg-spin, just as he knew everybody's Achilles' heel, and he brought himself on to deal with the England skipper. Douglas tried to hit against the spin and lobbed a dolly catch to slip. 'The stroke,' wrote Cardus, reporting his first Test match, 'must have been the ghastliest ever made in Test cricket by a responsible batsman.' As it transpired, Douglas was one of only four batsmen in the England innings to reach double figures. They were bowled out for 112. Gregory had 6 for 58, McDonald 3 for 42 and Armstrong 1 (Douglas) for 0. Australia made 232 and on the Monday afternoon, after less than two days cricket, they had won by ten wickets.

The Cricketer's reaction was to retain Douglas, Woolley, Knight and Hendren and replace the other seven with Hobbs, Hearne, A. J. Evans, A. P. F. Chapman, Smith, Parkin and Durston. The selectors came close to taking their advice. The four were retained, as was Strudwick, and A. J. Evans, Parkin and Durston came in, but Hobbs was still unfit and Dipper played, while places were found for Haig and Lionel Tennyson. Tennyson had been out of the picture since he toured South Africa with Douglas' side before the war, but he had been scoring runs for Hampshire and he had a romantic quality about him.

Douglas had batted with sterling courage in the second innings of the first Test and he showed resilience in the match at Lord's when, with Woolley, he tried to stem the Australian advance. He scored 34 and Woolley made 95. Dipper, 11, was the only other batsman to reach double figures. This time it was Mailey and McDonald who did the damage, and in the second innings, when Woolley scored 93 and Tennyson 74 not out, it was Gregory and McDonald. Douglas took 2 for 53 – he bowled only nine overs – and England were beaten by eight wickets. At least the game went into the third day.

Hobbs had been selected for the Lord's Test, but he had reported unfit and the selectors had asked C. B. Fry to play. Fry had agreed and had also agreed to play under Douglas to whom, of course, he was senior (Fry was then in his fiftieth year), but later he had withdrawn as he did not consider himself fit enough. It had also been intended that Fry should captain the MCC side against the Australians in May, but he had withdrawn from that match, too. Nevertheless, he was very much in the selectors' minds.

Douglas had now captained England in seven consecutive Test matches since the war and they had been beaten in every one of them. As any who have been concerned with the theatre will know, if you are going to have a good review and a bad review, it should happen that the bad review comes first, as then people will feel that you have improved. As a boxer, Douglas knew that what you did in the last round was often vital. His eight Test wins were history, his seven

Test defeats were current news. He had never had the total confidence of selectors who liked him as a man but doubted his tactical expertise as a captain. This was the first series in which he had ever been the selectors' first-choice captain, but even now, it was rumoured behind the scenes, that they had really wanted someone else – Fry perhaps, to rekindle the Golden Age.

It was not simply defeat that had undone Douglas, and indeed it is doubtful if the selectors (H. K. Foster, R. H. Spooner and J. Daniell) were themselves quite aware of what was happening. Their constant permutations in selection would certainly suggest that they had little idea of what was going on. Only in retrospect can we realise that Armstrong and his men were moving cricket into a new era, a post-war era of ruthless efficiency and tactical expertise when the psychological war became as important as the technique of the game. Armstrong brought a new dimension to field-placing, to probing at the batsman's weakness, to crowding, frustrating and attacking. Throughout the length and breadth of the country he was gaining the reputation of an ogre. He was a giant of a man and somehow the margin by which his side were winning, and the way in which they were winning, seemed not quite fair. It was of course perfectly fair, but the English cricket public was not quite ready for it. For them cricket was still heroics, not relentless efficiency. Tennyson was to give them their heroics, but he still lost.

Douglas was in between two worlds. In the Golden Age before the first world war, he had been a 'professional' amateur, lacking the panache, the flair, of the Jessops, the Frys, the Spooners and the rest. Yet that was the school in which he had learned his cricket. Now, in the post-war years, he was a relic from the Golden Age, full of dedication and unquenchable spirit, but out of his depth against a tactician like Armstrong. That he was hurt when he was deprived of the captaincy is undeniable, but the action could not have taken him greatly by surprise.

The clearest account of what happened is given by one of the men closest to the events, C. B. Fry:

I was playing for Hampshire just before the Lord's Test Match, and I had a brain-wave. I went up to London by an evening train and saw the selectors. I said to them that their difficulty was to find a batsman likely to knock off Gregory and Macdonald, who appeared to be on top of our batsmen. 'Take my advice,' I said, 'and play Lionel Tennyson. He is much more than a mere hitter. If he likes he can play proper cricket. He has a fine knack of hitting fast bowling. If you play him he may bat like a cow till he has made 15, fire a couple over slips' head, edge a couple between his legs and the wicket; but if he survives he will proceed to make 75 and you will have another Jessop.' They took my advice. Lionel Tennyson was played at Lord's. He did precisely what I had prophesied. He scored 74 not out. But we lost again.

The next move was that I should take on the captaincy at Leeds. To this I consented, having seen the English batsmen at Lord's and perceiving that I could not be less valuable than some of them against fast bowling. I consented because Hampshire were playing the Australians in the next few days and I could try myself out. I made 59 and 37, and none of their bowlers bothered me except Arthur Mailey, who, being one of the greatest of all leg-break bowlers, bothered other people as well. It happened that in this match Bardsley scored one of his left-handed double centuries. Just as he was on the edge of his second century it occurred to me that when he had registered it he would have a go. I guessed, too, that as he was not a straight driver he would have a go with his favourite square cut. So I crept in from deep square cover to backward point rather near in as that was where a mis-hit would go. Sure enough he did exactly what I had anticipated, and offered me a dolly sliced catch which I caught; but I caught it on the tip of my crooked little finger. With a damaged hand I did not care to take the field in a Test Match, so I had to cry off the Leeds match.

Thus it was that the selectors made Lionel Tennyson captain.

Douglas took his dismissal with the dignity that all who knew him had anticipated, and he stated that he was willing to serve under the new captain.

The irony was that Tennyson split a hand in the third Test and for a time Douglas was back in charge. There were similarities between the two men. They both lived well and played hard in a variety of sports. Socially, they were good companions, but Johnny was a much more dour, more serious figure on the field. They could both be colourful in their choice of language.

England lost the third Test, and with it the rubber. Tennyson played his heroic one-handed innings. Douglas took 3 for 80 and, in the first innings, scored 75, one of the finest innings by an English batsman during the series. There was a ray of light in the darkness of the English camp: although Hobbs, having been picked for the third Test, was stricken with appendicitis and unable to bat in either innings, the team had shown great spirit in spite of this handicap.

Tennyson was no more successful tactically than Douglas had been. His captaincy lacked subtlety and imagination and he was not to remain long in the job, but he had stirred some embers. The fourth Test was marred by rain and the fifth was drawn with England marginally having the better of things, but most people were glad when it was all over. The Australians were magnificent, but it is not too much fun to watch the heavyweight champion of the world knocking a street fighter around the ring for four months.

Douglas' personal contribution had been commendable. He and Woolley were the only players to represent England in all five Tests. He had played his first, and his last, Test matches against Australia in England. What was to come of his Test career was a postscript, but there were still some good years of cricket, and of living, to be had.

11
Recall

It was Frank Mann who led England to South Africa in 1922–23, and Johnny Douglas, at the age of 40, must have felt that his Test career was now behind him. It had no effect on his endeavour. Whether he was playing for England, Essex, the Gentlemen, C. I. Thornton's XI or H. D. G. Leveson-Gower's XI, he contested the match fiercely from beginning to end. He understood no other way. Everything was great fun. The social life after the match was full and hearty, but the match itself was deadly earnest.

G. O. Allen remembers a game in which Douglas was bowling to William Hill-Wood. Hill-Wood had scored quite a few runs, but most of them had been off the edge. When he edged one through the slips for four it was too much for Johnny, who flung his arms in the air and shouted down the wicket, 'When the bloody hell are you going to hit one in the middle, Willie?'

Hill-Wood smiled back down the wicket and said, 'The edge is good enough for you, Johnny.'

Douglas exploded. His face reddened and the air was blue. The next few deliveries were a little faster than usual, but at the end of it all he shared a bottle of vintage port with Hill-Wood that evening.

Douglas' reputation as a fearsome opponent became

legendary. His personality dominated the games in which he played and he was something of a law unto himself, striding the cricket world like a Colossus, so that it was a brave man who crossed him. In his last season, he was batting against Lancashire at Colchester. The wicket was rough and the Lancashire bowling was in the hands of Hodgson and McDonald. The Australian bounced one at Johnny which hit the handle of the bat and flew up to hit the batsman on the head. Douglas was felled like an ox, but the ball lobbed from his head into the hands of Harry Makepeace at cover. Nobody was very worried about Johnny being injured, because his toughness was well known, but they were worried as to who was going to break the news to him that he was out when he recovered.

The task was left to George Duckworth who tried to explain what had happened. Arthur Morton, the umpire, corroborated Duckworth's statement, and Johnny, fuming and swearing at Duckworth and everybody else in sight, stalked angrily from the field. In the evening the teams attended a reception at Colchester Town Hall. Douglas, among a crowd of players, attempted to win the Mayor's sympathy. 'I've played cricket a long time,' he said, 'but it's the first time I've been given out caught off my bloody head!' Dick Tyldesley, all innocence but with a twinkle in his eye, interrupted, 'Well, it certainly sounded like wood!' Johnny roared as if he had been struck again and chased Tyldesley the length of the Assembly Hall and out of the reception.

There were times when he could be reduced to silence. In the Gentlemen v. Players match at Lord's in 1924, he opened the bowling against Hobbs, who was captaining the Players. The wicket was lively and Hobbs made contact with only one ball in the opening over. Three times he was completely beaten and Douglas pounded the air as he whirled like a despairing Dervish. 'Well bowled, Colonel, well bowled,' called Hobbs. And then Douglas beat him again and it was the end of the over. Johnny stood in silent amazement at the tyranny of the gods. Hobbs went on to get a hundred.

This was the match in which Robertson-Glasgow, batting at no. 11, joined Douglas who was defying Tate and Howell in semi-darkness. Umpire Reeves took pity on the young man and suggested to him quietly that if he did not want to be killed, he should appeal against the light. Robertson-Glasgow took the advice and as the players left the field, Douglas was muttering and chuckling in amazement. 'Well,' he said, 'if that doesn't beat the bloody band; an appeal against the light by a number —— eleven! Why, I was just getting my eye in.'

Determination, tenacity, courage, these were the terms most often applied to Johnny Douglas. He never wanted to stop batting. He never wanted to stop bowling. He never wanted the game to end. He relished every contest and saw each one as a gladiatorial fight to the death. A. W. Carr, as captain and man a spiritual brother to Douglas, recalled him with the greatest admiration in his autobiography, *Cricket with the Lid Off*:

I liked him enormously, admired him enormously, and Johnnie and I were always good friends. I suppose in some ways he and I were rather like each other.

Johnnie Douglas was a determined, stand-no-nonsense chap. Some people did not take to him at first, but when you got to know him you discovered what was really in him. He was one of the greatest fighters in cricket I ever knew. I remember him playing in a match at Southend for Essex against Notts. Larwood, with the sea-breeze behind him, was bowling at a hell of a pace and Essex had about six wickets down for eighteen or so runs when Johnnie came in.

He said, 'No one will frighten me.' And for a long time we could not shift him. But he could not get a run and was out for 0. But in the second innings he came in again, also determined that no-one would frighten him – and again he was out for 0.

I could not help smiling but, all the same, I could not help admiring. In a tight corner I would as soon have had Johnnie Douglas on my side as anyone else I have ever met in the game.

The match to which Carr refers took place in 1927, but the determination would have been the same at any time in his career. R. C. Robertson-Glasgow described this quality in his *46 Not Out*:

> You knew, and could often hear, what he was thinking on the field. It was a battle, and nothing but, when he walked out, a gladiator, from the wicket gate, thick black hair shining and plastered down, rubbing the new ball on his strong forearm, frowning at some imaginary flaw in its make-up; or else went forth to bat, more grimly yet – for his batting was acquired and his bowling was natural – with strong slow gait, feet outwards, tugging his batting gloves on with his teeth, ready for a week, for a lifetime of that fight which was his cricket, and damn the bowlers and blast the crowd.

The image is a consistent one. He bristled with endeavour. 'His skill was great; but his courage, strength and enthusiasm were greater. His philosophy was simple – "Fight on!"'

And fight on he did. Essex finished eighth in 1922, but Douglas failed to score a century and failed to reach 1000 runs for the first time since 1913. The following season he had bounced back and he completed the double for what proved to be the last time. Inevitably, the best performance came when disaster threatened. Facing Gloucestershire's 324 on the first day of the Cheltenham Festival, Essex were in a desperate plight at 75 for 5. Douglas and O'Connor added 206 in 3½ hours and Essex went on to a great victory. The sixth-wicket record for the county has been equalled since but not surpassed.

For Essex, the 1924 season was the worst for many years and they finished fifteenth in the Championship table. For Douglas, the wet summer was a strange mixture. He limped through much of the season with a leg injury, scored only 733 runs, just reached his 100 wickets and was recalled to captain England. The recall took most people by surprise and was not received with universal approval although it was a temporary, emergency measure.

The South Africans were proving no match for an England side in which the bowling of skipper Gilligan and Maurice Tate was outstanding. Gilligan had taken 6 for 7 and Tate 4 for 12 in the first innings of the first Test when South Africa had been bowled out for 30. In the second Test, following wonderful batting by Hobbs, Sutcliffe and Woolley, Tate and Gilligan again bowled England to an innings victory. There was a similar pattern in the third Test which England won by nine wickets. Tate was the dominant bowler in this match, Gilligan having 1 for 27 and 0 for 37.

Ten days before this Test Gilligan had led the Gentlemen against the Players at the Oval. In the first innings he was struck a severe blow over the heart by a ball from Howell. He insisted on batting on and indeed, in the second innings he played a remarkable innings of 112 in an hour and a half as he and Falcon added 134 for the last wicket. The repercussions of that blow were great, though, and Gilligan was never again the same player. He withdrew from the fourth Test as he had suffered a reaction to the blow. Douglas was called in to act as substitute captain.

The Test itself was ruined by rain. South Africa were 116 for 4 when play was stopped and there were demonstrations by the Saturday crowd about the abandonment of play. Johnny Douglas' contribution to the match was eight overs and he also succeeded in impeding Geary when he was about to catch Ward at slip.

Three days before this Test began the first ten names of the England party to tour Australia in 1924–25 were announced. The team was to be led by Gilligan and it was stated that Frank Mann was not able to make the trip. Percy Chapman and J. L. Bryan were named among the first selections. At this stage no newspaper had seriously considered Douglas as a candidate for the tour, but when he was asked to lead the side after Gilligan's withdrawal from the match at Manchester rumours were rife, and during the inactive days of the Test it was officially announced that Douglas would go to Australia as vice-captain of the side. He was 42 years old and it was a surprising appointment. The reasoning behind it, seemingly, was that Douglas was to act as an elder statesman, advising and helping the younger players, but his own powers were undoubtedly in decline; 1924 was in fact the last season in which he was to take 100 wickets, and with the doubts that now existed about Gilligan's fitness, it was a strange choice.

Douglas, of course, accepted the position that he had been superseded in the captaincy by a man junior to himself who had not been before with an England side to Australia. Douglas' loyalty was unquestioned and it was to him that players turned for guidance. Sutcliffe had a loss of confidence before the first Test in Australia and sought help from Douglas. It was given readily: Douglas arranged a net practice in which he, Tate, Howell and 'Tich' Freeman mounted an attack on Sutcliffe which was not to end until the batsman felt that he had recaptured his form. It worked. Sutcliffe scored 59 and 115 in the first Test.

Douglas was liked and respected in Australia. He played cricket in a way that they understood. In the first game of the tour, at Perth, he was cheered all the way to the wicket. He made 22 in an hour which was described as 'painfully slow' in those days and went on to hit 62. In the second match of the tour, against Western Australia, he took his first wicket, the no. 9 Hewson. There were not to be many successes on the tour.

He was still cautious in his batting. He had 'never learned to let himself go,' complained Noble, but that was to miss the man. The essence was to resist the challenge, to do battle, and the determined digging in with the toe of the boot after he had taken guard was a gesture of hostility – they shall not pass. There was no room for the flamboyant stroke. That would have been a frivolity and batting was a serious business. He strained patience. He was dour, but he was never dull. There was too much character for that.

Naturally, his best innings of the tour came in the face of adversity. MCC were 143 for 6 against the strong Victorian side and things looked bad when Douglas came in. Noble wrote that Douglas' 59 not out was the finest innings he ever saw him play: 'a combination of sound defence and judicious hitting'. It could not save MCC from their first defeat of the tour, but it showed that the spirit was still there. It was in this match that Douglas took the wickets of Hartkopf and Wallace for a cost of 25 runs, and that turned out to be his best bowling performance of the tour.

He batted solidly as an opener against an Australian XI in Brisbane and scored 54, but he did not play in the first Test. Obviously, as vice-captain, he was one of the tour selectors and was party to his own non-selection. England were beaten by 193 runs and their greatest failing was that, against a strong Australian batting side on a perfect wicket, they had placed their attack almost entirely in the hands of three men, Gilligan, Tate and Freeman.

For the second Test, Freeman, rather cruelly, was replaced by Richard Tyldesley, and Sandham, lost at no. 6 or 7, was dropped in favour of Douglas. Collins won the toss and he and Bardsley opened against the bowling of Tate and

Douglas, Gilligan deferring to Douglas because of his vice-captain's ability to swing the new ball. Douglas bowled most economically, but without success, although at one time Australia were 47 for 3. Then Victor Richardson and Ponsford hit hundreds and Australia reached 600. Johnny Douglas dropped Richardson when he was on 67, and his bowling became more and more expensive. At the close he had Mailey lbw for 1. It was his last wicket in Test cricket and had cost him 95 runs.

Hobbs and Sutcliffe began with a stand of 283, but England trailed by 121 on the first innings. When Australia batted again, Tate and Hearne were the destroyers and Douglas bowled only four overs late in the innings. England needed 372 to win and, with Sutcliffe scoring 127, they were 211 for 3 at one stage, but they were beaten by 81 runs. Douglas came to the wicket when the score was 255 for 6 and it was ten to six on the sixth day. He stayed until the close. In Mailey's fourth over of the seventh morning, Sutcliffe misjudged the pitch of the ball and was caught at cover. Nine runs later Johnny Douglas was beaten and bowled by his old tormentor, Arthur Mailey, for 14, and he left the wicket in Test cricket for the last time. He had played in 12 Tests since the end of the war – three draws and nine losses. Those glorious successes of 1911–12 and 1913–14 were obscured by the mists of time.

As a bowler, a vital zest had left him. He was no longer impressive even with the new ball where once, in the opening overs, he had proved destructive. He had lost that mythical pace off the pitch. There had been some successes with the bat, but his six wickets on the tour, all of them lower-order batsmen, had cost 65.50 runs each.

12
The Sad Years

Although his days as a Test cricketer were now behind him, Johnny Douglas' commitment to Essex was far from over. The financial position of the county had been improved by the sale of the Leyton ground to the Army Sports Council in 1922, but the problems concerning the playing strength of the side persisted, and Douglas ruled his men as firmly and as fiercely as ever in his effort to bring better results.

There was, too, the business and social involvement with his father which remained as great as ever. Johnny Douglas was positive in everything that he did, and he always received the backing of his father. In return, he supported the family business which, after all, had made it possible for him to enjoy a good life. Old Douglas always maintained that his elder son did not really understand the timber trade, but he was good for business because of the position that he held in the sporting world.

It was the sporting world which provided the fabric for their social life. Douglas senior was the dominant force in the National Sporting Club and it provided the background for many glittering social occasions. Wanstead, the Douglases' club, was the venue for a match between Jimmy White's team and the National Sporting Club side (Jimmy White was a wealthy businessman and benefactor of many different sports). Hobbs, Parkin, Woolley, Russell,

119

Hendren, Gilligan and Douglas were among those who played in the pouring rain – an hour an innings for a one-pound bet. Douglas fielded with an umbrella and warmed everyone with his comments about playing cricket in such weather. The day finished with dinner at the National Sporting Club for 400 people.

Shortly after his return from Australia in 1925, Johnny Douglas and his father were on the Sportsmen's Table hosted by Jimmy White at the Prince of Wales' luncheon for the All Blacks. Parkin, Jimmy Wilde, Steve Donoghue, Billy Wells and many others were there at the Piccadilly Hotel. The non-attendance of Douglas, father and son, at such a gathering was unthinkable.

In the early 1920s, Johnny Douglas had moved to Theydon Bois where he lived in a splendid house named Colonsay which stands close to the golf course. He and his wife became well-known personalities in what was then little more than a village, although both tended to lead their separate lives. They had a red Armstrong Siddeley which, in those days when cars were a rarity, struck some awe into the local inhabitants.

On 7 January 1922, proposed by G. Buxton and seconded by F. Grimble, Johnny Douglas became a midweek member of Theydon Bois Golf Club. Less than a month later he was elected to full membership. G. O. Allen is of the opinion that Johnny Douglas was not a good golfer. He was stiff and there was no fluency in his swing but, as with all his success at other sports, what he achieved at golf he achieved through unrelenting determination. Within a year he won the club challenge cup and he won it again in 1928.

In 1923, Douglas proposed his stepson, Gerald, for membership of the golf club, but they rarely played together. Douglas was most anxious that the boy should learn the timber trade and succeed him in the family business. At first Gerald responded, and in the mid-1920s he joined the firm and went as its agent to Finland, from where Douglas and Sons imported their timber. He learned the language and, for a time, fought in the Finnish White Army, but he grew to believe that the timber trade was not for him. He returned to England in 1928 and announced that he wanted to go on the stage. Douglas' reaction was not unexpected: 'Damned boy! Blasted stage!'

'He came to see me once after I had got started,' says Gerald Case, 'and that was at the Camberwell Palace in 1929. He hated every minute of it and didn't disguise the fact although he said I was good in whatever small part I had.'

Undaunted, Gerald Case followed his stage career with success for over 50 years and now, at the age of 78, he makes occasional re-appearances. 'They always send for me when somebody's getting married in *Crossroads* and they need a vicar.'

Johnny Douglas became known more as a character than as a golfer. He would stride to the course for his game with his white bull-terrier, Sambo, at his heels. He controlled the dog with rather high-pitched hoots which it alone seemed to understand. He would bludgeon his way around the delightful little course and shout rude words at fellow members and friends, abusing them for their squeaking voices which were putting him off his game. None minded. The Colonel was accepted as a character. On the golf course, as on the cricket field, he was a law unto himself.

At the committee meeting on 20 February 1929, he was recommended for one of the vacancies on the committee, but he declined the invitation. In August of that year, he presented the club with a cup which was to be competed for in the October of each year. His stipulation was clear: 'Gentlemen play cricket until the 30th September, when they lay aside their pads and only then play golf.' The cup is competed for on the first week-end in October, two rounds on the Saturday and Sunday, and it is an eclectic, that is the best score over two holes. The original entrance fee of one shilling went to the Epping Cottage Hospital, and there was also a shilling sweepstake on the event. The original cup was lost and was replaced in 1931 by A. E. Jones, a friend and neighbour of Douglas' and his most frequent companion on the golf course. The cost of replacement was £5 5s 0d.

There are some at Theydon Bois Golf Club who still remember Johnny Douglas, and among them is Bob Dunn who caddied for Douglas when he was a boy. On the Friday evening the boys would sign the list to say that they wanted to caddy over the week-end. The fees were one shilling and two shillings for 'first-class' games, one penny of which was deducted by the club professional in return for emery paper with which the boys could clean the clubs belonging to those for whom they were caddying. Bob Dunn became a regular caddy for Douglas and A. E. Jones. Douglas was a rather awe-inspiring character and not all of the boys were too willing to caddy for him, but Bob found him straight and generous and respects the memory of the man. One Saturday, Bob Dunn had been caddying for Johnny Douglas, who said to him at the end of the round, 'We're playing at Chigwell tomorrow morning. Can you caddy?'

'Yes, sir,' said Dunn.

'Right. Be at my house at eight in the morning. You know where I live.'

Bob Dunn arrived at eight the next morning and was ushered into a front room. Douglas came in a few minutes later holding a glass of scotch. 'Here, son. Do you want this?' he asked, and handed the whisky to Bob Dunn.

Eleven years old and too frightened to refuse the great man, the boy drank the first scotch that he had ever tasted in his life at eight o'clock on a Sunday morning. 'He wasn't playing a trick on me,' says Bob Dunn. 'I'm sure of that. I think he just thought it was what a boy should have on a cold Sunday morning before he went out on the golf course.'

122

It was a gesture of the man whose generally brusque manner concealed a shyness and a sensitivity. The late Gordon Melluish played three games for Essex in 1926, and with very limited success. He remembered Douglas as a strong disciplinarian, with a manner which a young newcomer found forbidding, but then he gave Melluish a county cap, one of his own, as an encouragement.

Douglas' life was full of such 'little, nameless, unremembered acts of kindness and of love.' Yet somehow he was almost ashamed of them, as if they revealed some weakness. Those who were close to him, and most of those who played under him, were aware of them just as they were aware of the man's sheer strength of character and integrity. He never betrayed a principle in his life.

The fortunes of Essex revived considerably in 1925 and the side rose to seventh in the table, but Douglas' own form showed a marked decline. He scored more runs, 866, than he had done in 1924, but his bowling produced only 62 wickets, the fewest since he became captain of Essex. What was most marked was the decline in both speed and stamina. He was unable to bowl for long spells and his accuracy was far below the high standard that he had set. His pace deteriorated dramatically. There were comments and criticisms, but he said nothing. The increase in the county's fortunes distracted attention from the lack of success of the captain.

Typically, he had refused to admit that there was anything wrong with him. He abhorred any sign of weakness and he saw admitting to pain or illness as a weakness, but the truth was that for much of the 1925 season he was in considerable pain. The problem was diagnosed in the winter when he was operated upon for appendicitis. The recovery was slow and he could not take his place in the Essex side of 1926 until 21 July, when he led the team at Leyton in the match against Glamorgan. He did not bowl, but his presence had an inspirational effect and Glamorgan were beaten by six wickets, Douglas being at the crease when victory was obtained.

There were high hopes that he would now show a return to old form and lead Essex to triumphs. He hit 61 in the next match, a rain-ruined game with Middlesex, but again he did not bowl. He bowled four overs in the match with Lancashire and dismissed Harry Makepeace, but he was a ghost of his former self. His five wickets in the season cost 50 runs each, and the old fire had gone. As a captain he was forced to conserve his energies and that period of convalescent cricket must have been agony to him. Defiantly, in the last home match of the season, against Notts at Leyton, with Russell, Freeman, Hipkin and Eastman ill, he scored 103 in 3½ hours, but Essex lost by an innings.

In 1927, Johnny Douglas joined A. W. Carr and H. D. G. Leveson-Gower as an England selector, and the following year, with Lord Harris and 'Plum' Warner, they chose the side that was to go to Australia and win the series 4–1. As a selector, Douglas' record was as good as his early Test record had been.

He was now restored to full fitness, but not to full form. Incredibly, he scored over 1000 runs in 1927, but his batting had become totally introspective. Where once there had been defence of character, there now seemed to be defence of obsession. Scoring strokes were completely eschewed as if in pursuit of the fulfilment of some mission. The urgency of the rhythmical run had gone from his bowling and his pace was little more than slow. At times he even essayed a few would-be leg-breaks.

In the course of the season he selected 17 amateurs for the Essex side which, if it had the value of economy, had little to recommend it as a means of stabilising the side or producing the desired development in the professional staff who, naturally, murmured with discontent.

In the penultimate game of the season, at Scarborough, he hit his final century in first-class cricket, for MCC v. Yorkshire. The opponents and the venue were totally appropriate. He loved the Scarborough Festival. He played the cricket seriously and revelled in the good food and good wine and good table-talk in the evenings. They understood him in Yorkshire and, had they had the benefit of foresight, they would have realised that in that final century he was exacting his last revenge on them for the indignity that George Hirst had done to him 26 years earlier.

The second match of the Scarborough Festival was Gentlemen v. Players. Wilfred Rhodes captained the Players and Johnny Douglas captained the Gentlemen. It was the last time that either of them was to play in this fixture. They were the two greatest wicket-takers in these matches this century, and they left the scene together.

Few expected the following season, 1928, to show any great improvement for Essex, but few expected it to be quite as disastrous as it was. It was a summer drenched with sun and runs, but it was also the summer in which 'Tich' Freeman took 304 wickets and Ted McDonald 190. For Essex, it was a sad time. They won only two matches, against Somerset and Worcestershire, and only Worcestershire finished below them in the County Championship. In 32 matches, 39 players represented the county. 26 of them bowled. Jack O'Connor, with 68 wickets in all matches, was Essex's leading wicket-taker. Douglas himself took 22 wickets at a cost of 40.04 runs each. He bowled less and less. He was 46 years old and the engine was wearing. It comes to all; Douglas found it harder to accept than most.

At the end of July, at Leyton, he took 5 for 65 on a rain-affected pitch against Glamorgan. It was the one hundred and thirteenth time that he had taken five wickets in an innings. It was also the last time. He scored 848 runs in the season, but they were harder to come by, and even with the advantage of ten not outs, his average was only 21.74. Fielding had never been a strong point of the Essex game, but in 1928, it seemed to reach even lower depths and Douglas held frequent councils of war to underline this fact. He retained his fitness to the end of his life, but he was never a good fielder. There was a paradox in the man. He had a splendid physique, and his good bowling action and bounding run suggested a good athlete, but Douglas had acquired his prowess and nimble feet were not his. He did not look a good athlete in the field and his concern for the bad fielding of his side must have been tempered by the realisation of his own failing powers, but he still lived for Essex. His commitment to them, to his men, was total.

He wanted the success of others. Charles Bray remembers his maiden century. It was at the end of May 1928, against Middlesex at Leyton. Bray had batted no. 8 in the first innings, and when Essex went in again they trailed by 103 runs. As they were waiting for the start of the second innings Douglas approached Bray.

> Waiting until the last possible moment, he suddenly told me to go in first with, "I don't want to see you until tea-time." I made a hundred – my first, and the first is always the biggest thrill. John didn't come near me for a while. Of all the congratulations the ones I wanted most of all, the ones that meant more than all the others put together would come from him. He waited until I was alone in the dressing-room. Then he came in, put his hands on my shoulders, looked at me with his piercing eyes from under those shaggy eyebrows and said, "You see, I still had faith in you when you had lost faith in yourself. Well played," and turned and walked out of the room.

As the season progressed there were rumours of disquiet among the committee. There was talk of new leadership, a new approach. On 25, 27 and 28 August, Douglas led Essex against Leicestershire. He batted for an hour and three-quarters for 32 before Astill had him lbw. He got his revenge when he caught Astill, but he did not bowl in the Leicestershire innings. He was never to play for Essex again, for his battle with the committee had already begun.

He went up to Scarborough and in the opening match of the Festival, he scored 56 not out against Yorkshire when playing for MCC. It was his last fifty in first-class cricket.

He had been the virtual dictator of Essex cricket since the end of the war. He always did what he considered to be right, even if it might cause a temporary discomfort. Sometimes he was wrong, but more often he was right; for he was no man for compromises or half-measures. In whatever he did, he had the full support of his father. The committee made suggestions to Johnny Douglas, but he made the decisions.

At the end of the 1928 season, the committee suggested to Douglas that he should resign as they felt that a change of captaincy was desirable. They intended that H. M. Morris should succeed him as captain. Douglas refused to resign, mainly because he considered that the committee's choice of his successor was wrong. He felt that Morris was lacking in commitment to the county and the events of the next few years proved him to be right. Morris rarely played a full season, and Essex were not to have a regular captain until the 1933 season.

Douglas fought the committee with the same tenacity that he had fought his battles on the cricket field, but this was a battle he was destined to lose. It was a sad business, badly managed. The man had given his life to Essex, carrying them on his broad shoulders for 18 years. In his personal achievements he had brought them honours which none had brought them before. It was service that demanded respect and that respect was absent.

Perhaps he had been so long the dictator, one whom it needed courage to approach, that the committee had lost all sense of tact in how to deal with such a situation as had now arisen. Certainly he had not become easier with the years: his enthusiasm was as great as ever, his eagerness phenomenal for one who had tasted so much, but time erodes physical ability and he found it difficult to face the failings in himself and blamed others.

The conflict between captain and committee became a bitter one, and the cricket world gaped in horror at the open wounds. The committee sent a deputation to Douglas at his office in the City. The party was headed by a solicitor for whom Johnny Douglas had a particular dislike. He refused to see them. On Monday 3 December 1928, the committee met for an hour and a half to discuss the matter of captaincy. At the close of the meeting, the secretary, Mr G. H. Thompson, issued a statement: 'Mr H. M. Morris has been asked to captain the Essex County Cricket Club for next season and he has accepted the post. It is very much hoped that the valuable services of Mr J. W. H. T. Douglas will be available as a playing member of the team.' Two days later, Douglas issued a statement saying that he had no intention of retiring from first-class cricket. *The Times* hinted that he had a birth qualification for Middlesex. Murmurs and mutterings continued. It was a sad time.

On Christmas Eve, Essex County Cricket Club issued a statement which was published in the newspapers of 27 December:

> It is with reluctance my committee have decided to give publicity to the circumstances under which a change in the captaincy of the Essex County Cricket Club was made. In view, however, of the accounts appearing in the Press recently and in justice to the members of the club and the cricket public in general, they feel it is incumbent upon them to make the following statement –

The committee of the club have been aware for some considerable time that there was a feeling in the county that a change in the captaincy was desirable. When this became very evident at the close of last season, three members of the committee, including myself, called upon Mr Douglas at his office in September and explained to him the situation and asked him whether, in the circumstances, he would resign. He informed us that he would consider this but added that if the committee thought that they would like a change, they should certainly make it.

Mr Douglas attended a meeting of the committee on November 5, when the question of the captaincy was discussed. At this meeting it was decided to refer the matter to the cricket sub-committee for further consideration and report. This sub-committee, of which Mr Douglas is a member, met on November 12, but Mr Douglas regretted his inability to be present. This meeting, after very fully considering the whole question, decided to recommend that such a change was desirable. The general committee met on December 3 when the recommendation of the cricket sub-committee was fully considered and adopted. Due notice of this meeting was sent to Mr Douglas, but he regretted he was once again unable to attend. Minutes were sent to Mr Douglas very soon after each meeting.

The meetings were not secretive, as has been suggested in some quarters, but were properly constituted meetings of the committee held in the board room of the club's honorary solicitors where for years past business has been transacted in the winter months.

I hope it will, therefore, be clear that the appointment of Mr Morris as the new captain was not made without very full and earnest consideration by the committee, nor without Mr Douglas being made fully aware of the fact.

Mr Douglas states there has been disloyalty towards him by certain members of the team. This fact the committee were fully aware of, and it weighed with them in coming to their decision.

Nobody is more fully aware of the wonderful services Mr

Douglas has rendered to the game of cricket than the committee, or more grateful to him for his services, and it was with deep regret and only after anxious consideration that it was decided to make the change. Mr Douglas has been asked to play as often as possible for the team and to become a member of the selection committee, and it is the earnest wish of the committee that he will do both.

(Signed) C. STEWART RICHARDSON
Chairman, Essex County Cricket Club.
December 24, 1928

In an effort to make peace they made J. W. H. T. Douglas a life member in 1929, but he never played for them again, neither did Perrin, nor Freeman, nor Gillingham. It was the end of an era, and nothing that ever happened in his life affected Johnny Douglas as much as the break with the county to whom he had given his life and his love.

13
Passion Spent

As he had promised, John Douglas did not retire from first-class cricket. He played ten matches in 1929, six of them for MCC, including the match against the South African touring team. He was at the Scarborough Festival to play for MCC against Yorkshire and although he bowled very little during the season, he still revealed those fine qualities of batting, concentration and defence. He maintained his own personal definition of an optimist as 'a man who, batting with Johnny Douglas, backs up for a run'.

He still loved the game. It was still a great battle and a great social occasion. In March 1929, he had added further to his tours by making a brief visit to Malta with an Incogniti team which included P. T. Eckersley, J. C. W. MacBryan, T. Arnott and H. D. G. Leveson-Gower. It was a friendly, happy tour, with two defeats and a draw against the service opposition. Douglas scored 40 not out in the first match on the Marsa Cricket Ground, and he took the wicket of Captain C. G. B. Stevens in the second match. The cricket was enjoyable; the entertainment was magnificent.

He played less in 1930, only four matches. In May, playing for MCC against Surrey at Lord's, he bowled Shepherd in the second innings. It was his last wicket in first-class cricket. He played for Leveson-Gower's XI against both universities at Eastbourne and, at Lord's on 20,

21 and 22 August, he played for MCC against Wales in his last appearance in first-class cricket. He led an MCC side which included the young Nawab of Pataudi, Astill, the South African, Pegler, and R. H. R. Buckston, later to lead Derbyshire. Pataudi scored 105. Douglas was lbw to Arnott for 1.

Pegler and Astill bowled Wales out for 67. There was no play on the Thursday because of rain, but Pegler and Pickthall bowled them out a second time for 154 on the Friday. Douglas took one catch, his old colleague S. F. Barnes to whom he had denied the new ball in Sydney 19 years earlier, but that misjudgment had long been forgiven.

All passion was spent in his duel with Fender. On 16 October, they both attended a farewell gathering for the MCC side that Percy Chapman was taking to South Africa. The function was given by the Union Castle Company at Southampton. Fender and Douglas were the sole occupants of a compartment on the train back to London that evening, and Fender is quoted by his biographer, Dick Streeton, as saying that something of a *rapprochement* took place between the two men. The struggle was over.

> Nothing happened that you could put a finger on exactly but we talked about all sorts of things, including Australia in 1920–21. For the first time we seemed to get close. We were still talking when we got to London and he asked me to go and have a drink – and we had several together. In all the years we had known each other nothing like it happened before. We were both past being competitive by then and this may have helped, but when we parted we both felt, I think, that any past differences between us were finished. It can happen that way with people you have had a bit of a feud with.

In the months ahead, Fender was grateful for that evening.

132

The way in which the business of J. H. Douglas and Company worked was that old Douglas and one of his sons would journey to Scandinavia in the winter and purchase timber which would be delivered when the ports became unfrozen in the spring. The timber, as mentioned earlier, was used for making the staves in which cement was kept and sold. Before the winter trip of 1930 Frank Mann and Nigel Haig arranged a special dinner in Johnny Douglas' honour at the International Sportsman's Club. G. O. Allen remembers it well as a fine occasion. 'Frank Mann was not one to arrange things like that lightly. He would not have done it for everybody, but they wanted to do it for Johnny.'

It was a miserable winter, that winter of 1930, with thick fog blanketing much of Northern Europe for long periods. Fog hung over the Meuse Valley at the beginning of December, bringing death to 64 people. There were fog accidents in London and much of the world seemed gripped by it. Old Douglas had retired as head of the firm and Johnny had succeeded him, but the old man still held the reins in many ways and went with his son to Finland to buy the timber for the delivery in 1931. They negotiated the business in Finland and were returning to England in a Finnish ship, the *Oberon*, which they hoped would bring them home in time for Christmas.

The *Oberon*'s captain was Erik Hjelt, and he took his wife and eight-year-old daughter with him on the voyage from Helsinki to Hull so as to celebrate Christmas together on board. His brother, Ossi, was captain of the *Oberon*'s sister ship, *Arcturus*, which was bound from Hull to Helsinki and, like his brother, Captain Ossi Hjelt had his wife accompanying him.

At the start of the voyage the *Oberon* was in a minor collision with another Finnish steamer in the Baltic Sea while they were exchanging mailbags, but she continued her voyage. The *Oberon* and the *Arcturus* were due to pass each other at the entrance to the Kattegat late on 19 December. The two captains exchanged Christmas greetings by wireless. There was hope that the ships would pass within sight of each other and that the brothers would be able to wave a greeting, but the fog became dense. It appears that even after their exchange of messages the brothers did not realise how close their ships were to each other, but Captain Erik Hjelt at least had some idea, for he was sounding the ship's siren when the *Arcturus* loomed out of the fog on starboard side. A collision was unavoidable.

The *Oberon* was stove in on the starboard side from midships to stern. In half a minute she had a list of something like 30 degrees, and three minutes later she had sunk. 42 people went down with the *Oberon*, including 18 of the 22 passengers.

None can be sure what happened in those last moments. The official enquiry revealed that the first-class passengers were gathered in the saloon at the time of the collision. There were reports that old Douglas was in his cabin and his son went from the saloon to the cabin and was not seen again. But in a sworn affidavit, Mr Ernest Martin, a timber merchant who lived in Helsinki and whose wife Mary was drowned, stated that John Douglas went on deck when the *Arcturus* rammed them. Douglas and Mr and Mrs Martin made their way to the port side with some difficulty and saw old Douglas standing at the top of the stairs leading to the smoke-room. They implored the old man not to go below, but he gestured as if he were going to collect something. John went to him at the top of the stairs. In doing so, he undoubtedly relinquished what chance he had of saving his own life. He was never seen again. J. W. H. T. Douglas had fought his last battle with the elements.

14
Postscript

The news of the death of John Douglas came as a profound
shock to the cricket world. Like him or loathe him, you
could not ignore him.

Sir Pelham Warner read of the news in an evening paper in
South Africa.

> For a second or two my heart stopped beating. John had
> served me so well in Australia in 1911–12 when I was laid
> aside by illness, and it was hard to realise that so vital and
> strong a life had gone. Father and son were devoted to each
> other, their relationship was a beautiful one – and if John had
> to die, I imagine he would have sought no finer end.

On Monday 29 December, the General Purposes Committee
of the Amateur Boxing Association stood in silence for two
minutes before their meeting at 22 Great St James Street. It
was their tribute to two men who had done much for them.

At Whitsun 1933, P. R. Wilson, President of the Old
Felstedian Society and a governor of the school, dedicated a
pavilion at Felsted School to the memory of the school's
greatest cricketer. The pavilion was constructed from a
group of converted cottages which stood between Elwyn's
and The Chequers. It was named the Douglas Pavilion.

There were memorial services for father and son. Lord

Harris, Sir Home Gordon, Leveson-Gower, Ronnie Aird, G. T. S. Stevens and Herbert Strudwick were among those present at St Michael's, Cornhill on 30 December, but perhaps the most moving tribute was that paid by Rev. Frank Gillingham at St Mary's Parish Church, Leyton. In his address, John Douglas' old team-mate said that his friend had been an inspiration to all men, and particularly to the young. He emphasised four qualities in Douglas' life that were a model for all.

Firstly, there was his modesty. Never in the years that Gillingham knew Douglas did he hear him refer to his success at boxing, nor did he ever draw attention to his own prowess in any field. He was silent upon those deeds which had made him great.

Secondly, there was his dogged determination. He refused to be beaten and there was a whole-hearted perseverance in everything that he did. He was not a natural games player, but many men who were far more gifted than he lacked the concentration and application that he possessed, and so failed to approach his standard. He never gave up in his own mind. He had achieved success through thorough hard work.

Douglas' loyalty to his friends was the third quality to which Gillingham drew attention. 'I said when he was living,' Gillingham said, 'and I say again now that he is dead, that if I had my back to the wall and was in trouble, I would rather have John Douglas alongside me than any other man.'

The last point was well known to all – John's devotion to his father. The father worshipped the son and gave him every chance to succeed. In return, the son repaid the father with complete devotion and always ascribed all his success to his father. He was a modest man, loyal to his friends, devoted to his father, fearless in opposition and generous in success. He and his father were 'lovely and pleasant in their lives, and in their death they were not divided.'

There were simpler tributes. 46 years after John Douglas'
death, Arthur H. Wagg, the former statistician and Essex
enthusiast, could write to Leslie Newnham:

> I saw J.W.H.T. in the field many times in the 20's at Leyton.
> Among the performances which have stuck in my mind were
> the beautiful break-back with which he bowled Plum
> Warner in the game in which Essex beat Middlesex by four
> runs. On another occasion he had to calm down a section of
> the crowd who objected to F. T. Mann's hitting for 4 a ball
> which (I think) C. T. Ashton let slip and which came to rest
> half way down the pitch. He was also very scathing towards
> A. B. Hipkin on one occasion when he took the field with a
> cigarette in his mouth.
>   I was on the point of tears when the news of his death by
> drowning became known.

There were other, less generous, tributes. All that the Essex
County Year Book of 1931 could find to say of the man who
had been the backbone of the county for nearly twenty years
was 'It is with very deep regret that your Committee have to
record the deaths of Mr J. H. Douglas, a past President and
serving member of the Committee: Mr J. W. H. T. Douglas,
for so many years Captain: and of Sir Joseph Hood, Bart,
one of the Club's Vice-Presidents.' Nevertheless, they flew
the flags at Leyton at half-mast when he died. Alan Gibson
remembers them as the first flags that he ever saw flying at
half-mast and says that he cannot see a flag flown this way
today without remembering Johnny Douglas.

Wisden felt that with his cramped style and limited number
of strokes, he could never be described as an attractive
player, although his bowling was far more interesting and
his stamina quite magnificent.

Sir Home Gordon's attack was to come nine years after
John Douglas' death, but even though he qualified every
assessment with a vitriolic comment, Home Gordon had to

admit that 'his dogged enthusiasm for cricket was unsurpassable' and that his epitaph must be that 'he was gallant and unsparing as well as keen.'

His relentless devotion to what he believed to be right and his devotion to his friends were the qualities chiefly remembered.

There was a legend that his last appearance in the ring was a three-round exhibition bout with Gunner Moyes and he was disqualified – wrongly, he felt. He would never query a referee's decision, but he would never fight again. It is an apocryphal story, but then all apocryphal stories are born of character and thrive because they have a ring of truth, or what we would like to believe to be true.

Perhaps there is an appropriate time for death, and 19 December 1930, near the island of Laesoe, was an appropriate time for Douglas. In the spring of 1931, the cement manufacturers decided to store their produce in paper sacks rather than in staves which J. H. Douglas and Company had produced for them for nearly 50 years. It was lighter, it was cheaper, it was progress. With 'Pickles' at the helm, the firm struggled on until the outbreak of the second world war, when its death knell was finally sounded. It was as well that John Douglas was spared the death of the firm. The end of his affiliation with his beloved Essex had broken his heart, and the end of one's days should not be all decline and despair.

As early as 1922, 'Pickles' had refereed the George Cook v. Joe Beckett fight, and in the 1930s he was the leading referee in England. As a referee, he gained a reputation like the one his brother had gained as a cricket captain, 'a bit of a martinet', but he controlled with fairness and humour the Carnera v. Cook fight in 1932, Doyle v. Petersen in 1933, both the Harvey v. Petersen fights, Harvey v. Neusel, and many others which involved leading British boxers. He spent his last days in Frinton-on-Sea where he died in 1954 at the age of 68. Following the decline of the family business, he had worked for the Clacton District Council, mainly in jobs like sweeping and tidying, but defiantly cheerful to the end. There was something indestructible about the Douglases.

The name still reverberates around the cricket grounds of Essex and England, and many who were not born when the *Oberon* sank in the Kattegat know the nickname of an England captain who gained a reputation for slow scoring that tended to obscure his qualities as a bowler. His end with Essex was not a happy one, but his memory is loved and revered today. Without him and his father, it is likely that Essex would not have survived.

'Tiny' Waterman, the present chairman of the club, and one whom Johnny Douglas first encouraged to play, gave me much help in the preparation of this study. After a discussion in the committee room which overlooks the ground at Chelmsford, I got up to leave. On reaching the door, I was called back by 'Tiny' Waterman. The chairman hesitated. There was something he wanted to add without wanting it to be thought that he was dictating what must be written. He smiled. 'When you write of him,' he said, 'just say that we owe him so much.'

Appendix

J. W. H. T. Douglas' Career Statistics

Compiled by Leslie Newnham

FIRST-CLASS MATCHES: BATTING AND FIELDING

Season	Matches	Inns	NO	Runs	HS	Ave.	100s	50s	0s	Ct
1901	3	5	1	69	61*	17.25	—	1	3	—
1903	16	27	3	300	54	12.50	—	1	2	16
1904	24	37	7	526	66	17.53	—	2	9	13
1905	17	30	4	510	79*	19.61	—	3	4	11
1906	25	44	5	1015	98	26.02	—	7	8	19
1906–07 New Zealand	9	14	3	398	67	36.18	—	2	1	7
1907	27	50	6	992	69*	22.54	—	3	5	16
1907–08 United States	2	4	0	47	39	11.75	—	—	1	—
1908	28	41	4	1167	115	31.54	2	6	1	13
1909	28	50	2	998	102	20.79	1	5	8	16
1910	24	46	4	965	79	22.97	—	5	4	17
1911	25	46	3	1279	176	29.74	1	6	4	18

1911–12 Australia	12	15	3	416	140	34.66	2	—	3	5
1912	29	46	2	1411	129	32.06	2	8	3	12
1913	23	41	4	543	88	14.67	—	1	8	11
1913–14 South Africa	18	21	5	827	119	51.68	2	6	1	12
1914	25	39	3	1288	146	35.77	2	7	1	15
1919	28	43	9	1178	144	34.64	2	3	1	14
1920	30	48	7	1328	147	32.39	2	6	4	15
1920–21 Australia	13	18	4	816	133*	58.28	3	6	2	5
1921	30	49	8	1547	210*	37.73	—	7	—	25
1922	30	47	6	979	84	23.78	2	3	4	16
1923	30	48	10	1110	147*	29.21	1	1	1	10
1924	29	43	12	733	102*	23.64	—	—	3	15
1924–25 Australia	8	11	2	239	62	26.55	—	3	1	4
1925	26	38	7	866	68*	27.93	—	4	2	16
1926	13	20	5	528	103	35.20	1	3	2	6
1927	33	47	13	1295	101*	38.08	1	4	3	16
1928	32	49	10	848	68*	21.74	—	5	5	10
1929	10	13	3	287	42*	28.70	—	—	—	6
1930	4	5	1	26	11	6.50	—	—	—	3
Career total	651	1035	156	24531	210*	27.90	26	108	94	362

Matches in Great Britain

For Essex:

County Championship (1901–28)	437	706	101	16927	210*	27.97	17	73	62	252
Other matches (1905–28)	22	40	7	988	129	29.93	1	5	4	13
Total for Essex	459	746	108	17915	210*	28.07	18	78	66	265

Season	Matches	Inns	NO	Runs	HS	Ave.	100s	50s	0s	Ct
England – Tests (1912–24)	7	9	1	218	75	27.25	—	1	—	4
An England XI (1909–29)	2	1	0	102	102	102.00	1	—	—	2
Gentlemen v. Players (1906–27)	30	56	7	757	72	15.44	—	2	7	15
Gentlemen of England (1907–19)	4	7	1	273	94	45.50	—	3	—	3
Gentlemen of the South (1909)	1	2	0	29	15	14.50	—	—	—	1
MCC (1907–30)	38	60	7	1282	101*	24.18	1	1	4	13
MCC Australian Team (1911–25)	4	5	1	128	68*	32.00	—	1	1	—
MCC South African Team (1914)	1	2	0	30	16	15.00	—	—	—	—
South v. North (1905–08)	3	5	1	113	86*	28.25	—	1	1	2
South of England (1909)	1	2	0	22	20	11.00	—	—	—	—
The Rest – Test trial (1912)	1	2	0	34	24	17.00	—	—	—	—
Rest v. Champion County (1912–24)	5	5	2	160	69*	53.33	—	1	—	5
London County (1903–04)	11	19	2	275	66	16.17	—	2	4	8
Lord Londesborough's XI (1908–12)	4	5	1	44	26	11.00	—	—	2	2
H. D. G. Leveson Gower's XI (1914–30)	9	13	4	183	45	20.33	—	—	—	3
C. I. Thornton's XI (1919–27)	5	7	3	104	61	26.00	—	1	—	3
L. Robinson's XI (1919–21)	2	3	1	54	41*	27.00	—	—	—	1
Free Foresters (1919–29)	2	3	0	65	31	21.66	—	—	—	2
Total in Great Britain	589	952	139	21788	210*	26.79	20	91	85	329
Matches in Australia										
England (1911–25)	11	19	1	478	68	26.55	—	4	2	3
MCC (1911–25)	22	25	8	993	140	58.41	4	5	4	11
Total in Australia	33	44	9	1471	140	42.02	4	9	6	14

Matches in South Africa

	M	I	NO	Runs	HS	Ave	100	50	St	Ct
England (1913–14)	5	7	0	266	119	38.00	1	1		2
MCC (1913–14)	13	14	5	561	102*	62.33	1	5	—	10
Total in South Africa	18	21	5	827	119	51.68	2	6	1	12

Matches in New Zealand

	M	I	NO	Runs	HS	Ave	100	50	St	Ct
MCC (1906–07)	9	14	3	398	67	36.18	—	2	1	7

Matches in United States of America

	M	I	NO	Runs	HS	Ave	100	50	St	Ct
MCC (1907)	2	4	0	47	39	11.75	—	—	1	—

Highest score: 210* for Essex v. Derbyshire at Leyton, 1921.
Best Season: 1547 runs (ave. 37.73) in 1921.

FIRST-CLASS MATCHES: BOWLING

Season	Overs		Mdns	Runs	Wkts	Ave.	5wI	10wM	Best
	6-ball	8-ball							
1901	—	—	—	—	—	—	—	—	—
1903	204.1	—	39	668	25	26.72	1	—	5–63
1904	367.5	—	63	1187	37	32.08	—	—	4–37
1905	255.5	—	46	904	35	25.82	3	—	5–31
1906	626.4	—	113	2144	93	23.05	5	1	8–33
1906–07 New Zealand	239.3	—	51	663	50	13.26	5	1	7–49
1907	572.1	—	98	1863	90	20.70	5	2	7–86
1907–08 United States	15.3	—	0	53	3	17.66	—	—	3–42
1908	637.1	—	74	2202	83	26.53	5	1	6–29

Season	Overs 6-ball	8-ball	Mdns	Runs	Wkts	Ave.	5wI	10wM	Best
1909	443.4	—	63	1522	65	23.41	3	—	7–75
1910	329.5	—	47	1091	56	19.48	—	—	4–17
1911	645.5	—	93	2049	82	24.98	1	—	5–53
1911–12 Australia	316.5	—	71	803	37	21.70	2	—	5–46
1912	709.1	—	137	2188	81	27.01	3	—	7–39
1913	566	—	83	1780	68	26.17	3	—	5–40
1913–14 South Africa	179.4	—	30	531	30	17.70	—	—	4–14
1914	789.2	—	121	2636	138	19.10	13	4	9–105
1919	968	—	135	3420	136	25.14	11	2	8–49
1920	925.2	—	154	3144	147	21.38	10	1	8–39
1920–21 Australia	260.2	—	33	918	27	34.00	2	—	7–98
1921	850.2	—	147	2642	130	20.32	9	4	9–47
1922	845	—	157	2518	109	23.10	5	2	8–45
1923	976.4	—	166	3257	146	22.30	14	4	8–90
1924	749.3	—	163	2067	102	20.26	8	1	7–66
1924–25 Australia	—	100.1	10	393	6	65.50	—	—	2–25
1925	599.3	—	133	1590	62	25.64	2	—	5–52
1926	87	—	16	250	5	50.00	—	—	3–61
1927	281.5	—	66	721	27	26.70	2	—	5–52
1928	314.4	—	52	881	22	40.04	1	—	5–65
1929	10	—	1	32	0	—	—	—	—
1930	14	—	1	42	1	42.00	—	—	1–42
Career total	13781.2	100.1	2363	44159	1893	23.32	113	23	9–47

Matches in Great Britain

For Essex:

County Championship	10043.3	1723	31804	1375	23.13	92	20	9–47
Other Matches	509.2	77	1849	68	27.19	1	1	7–50
Total for Essex	10552.5	1800	33653	1443	23.32	93	21	9–47
England – Tests	102	12	368	11	33.45	—	—	3–80
An England XI	10	0	68	1	68.00	—	—	1–68
Gentlemen v. Players	663.2	100	2216	90	24.62	5	1	9–105
Gentlemen of England	161.4	35	407	24	16.95	—	—	4–22
Gentlemen of the South	15	2	51	4	12.75	—	—	4–18
MCC	533.2	89	1636	74	22.10	3	—	6–65
MCC Australian Team	91	17	347	9	38.55	—	—	2–38
MCC South African Team	25	2	87	1	87.00	—	—	1–87
South v. North	40	2	183	2	91.50	—	—	1–17
South of England	25.2	2	75	7	10.71	1	—	7–75
The Rest – Test trial	10	1	38	0	—	—	—	—
Rest v. Champion County	120.5	32	324	21	15.42	1	—	7–39
London County	113.3	21	382	15	25.46	—	—	4–103
Lord Londesborough's XI	65	18	167	5	33.40	—	—	3–44
H. D. G. Leveson Gower's XI	50	6	149	6	24.83	—	—	2–20
C. I. Thornton's XI	64.3	10	176	7	25.14	—	—	3–55
L. Robinson's XI	68.5	12	227	13	17.46	1	—	6–64
Free Foresters	57.2	7	244	7	34.85	—	—	4–40
Total in Great Britain	12769.3	2168	40798	1740	23.44	104	22	9–47

	Overs		Mdns	Runs	Wkts	Ave.	5wI	10wM	Best
	6-ball	8-ball							
Matches in Australia									
England	251.5	23.5	43	879	24	36.62	1	—	5–46
MCC	325.2	76.4	71	1235	46	26.84	3	—	7–98
Total in Australia	577.1	100.1	114	2114	70	30.20	4	—	7–98
Matches in South Africa									
England	74.2	—	11	239	10	23.90	—	—	4–14
MCC	105.2	—	19	292	20	14.60	—	—	4–26
Total in South Africa	179.4	—	30	531	30	17.70	—	—	4–14
Matches in New Zealand									
MCC	239.3	—	51	663	50	13.26	5	1	7–49
Matches in United States of America									
MCC	15.3	—	0	53	3	17.66	—	—	3–42

Best bowling: 9–47 for Essex v. Derbyshire at Leyton, 1921
Best match analysis: 14–91 for Essex v. Hampshire at Bournemouth, 1921
Best season: 147 wickets (ave. 21.38) in 1920.

TEST MATCHES FOR ENGLAND

Batting and Fielding	Matches	Inns	NO	Runs	HS	Ave.	100s	50s	0s	Ct
v. Australia (1911–25)	17	28	2	696	75	26.76	—	5	2	7
v. South Africa (1913–24)	6	7	0	266	119	38.00	1	1	1	2
Test career total	23	35	2	962	119	29.15	1	6	3	9

Highest score: 119 v. South Africa at Durban (1st Test), 1913–14.

Bowling	Overs		Mdns	Runs	Wkts	Ave.	5wI	10wM	Best
	6-ball	8-ball							
v. Australia	345.5	23.5	53	1227	35	35.05	1	—	5–46
v. South Africa	82.2	—	13	259	10	25.90	—	—	4–14
Test career total	428.1	23.5	66	1486	45	33.02	1	—	5–46

Best bowling: 5–46 v. Australia at Melbourne (4th Test), 1911–12.

Index

148

149

152